Discipleship Lessons from the
Life of Jacob

A Bible Study Commentary on Genesis 25-49

for Personal Devotional Use, Small Groups or
Sunday School Classes, and Sermon Preparation for Pastors and Teachers

JesusWalk® Bible Study Series

by Dr. Ralph F. Wilson
JesusWalk® Bible Study Series

Additional books, and reprint licenses are available at:
www.jesuswalk.com/books/jacob.htm

Free Participant Guide handout sheets are available at:
www.jesuswalk.com/jacob/jacob-lesson-handouts.pdf

JesusWalk® Publications
Loomis, California

Copyright © 2010, Ralph F. Wilson. All rights reserved. May not be copied or reproduced without explicit permission.

Paperback
ISBN-13: 978-0-9819721-4-5
ISBN-10: 0981972144

Library of Congress Control Number: 2009913870

Library of Congress subject headings:
Jacob (Biblical patriarch)
Bible. O.T. Genesis XXVI-L
Bible. O.T. Genesis
Bible study guide

Suggested Classifications
Dewey Decimal System: 222.11
Library of Congress: BS580

Published by JesusWalk® Publications, P.O. Box 565, Loomis, CA 95650-0565, USA.

JesusWalk is a registered trademark and Joyful Heart is a trademark of Joyful Heart Renewal Ministries.

Unless otherwise noted, all the Bible verses quoted are from the New International Version (International Bible Society, 1973, 1978), used by permission.

100105

Preface

Jacob is a troubling character in the Old Testament. He is conniving and he is spiritual too. He has moments of strong faith as well as of fear. His family is sometimes in disarray, and yet at the end he is the one who sets it straight.

Jacob, whose very name suggests "deceiver," is re-named by God as "Israel" – "one who has struggled with God." And an entire nation is named after him, the nation of Israel.

Jacob is a bit too much like us, with very human strengths and weaknesses, but a man with a striving for spiritual things.

From this imperfect man we learn important lessons of faith. Especially, we learn about God's grace.

The events described in Jacob's story comprise most of Genesis chapters 25-49. If you haven't read the Old Testament much, you'll be pleased to find that God can speak to you here – loud and clear. Try to accept the fact that the culture described here is nearly 4,000 years ago and they did things differently then. But you'll quickly see that the people and their problems haven't changed much.

James J. Tissot, "Jacob" (c. 1896-1902), gouache on board, 24.4 x 12.3 cm, Jewish Museum, New York.

The story of Jacob is a great opportunity to learn important lessons about ourselves and our God.

This is not the kind of Bible study for the faint of heart. We'll be looking at some issues that don't have nice, neat answers. But life is like that. You'll grow through this process. You'll become closer to, more sensitive to, more obedient to God – plus you'll learn to study your Bible in a new way.

I originally wrote this in 1998 as an early attempt at online Bible study. Since then, it has been completely revised, annotated, and adapted for an interactive e-mail Bible study, complete with discussion questions that can be used by individuals in an online forum, as well as by classes and small groups. The questions are designed to force you to grapple with the core issues and spiritual lessons that lie a little below the surface. I encourage you to take the time to answer these questions, as they are one of the keys to a deeper understanding and application of the material.

My prayer is that you will grow in your faith as you study the Life of Jacob. I know God has challenged my life in the course of my studies. I pray he will challenge and refine your life, too.

Yours in Christ's service,
Dr. Ralph F. Wilson
Loomis, California
January 1, 2010

Table of Contents

Preface	3
Table of Contents	5
Reprint Guidelines	9
Online Bible Study Forum	10
References and Abbreviations	11
Introduction to Jacob's Life and Times	**12**
Jacob's Life in a Nutshell	12
Yahweh and the Religions of the Ancient Near East	13
The Patriarchs' Religion	14
Authorship of Genesis and the Pentateuch	15
Dating of Jacob	15
Chronology of Jacob	16
Chief Places Jacob Lived	18
1. Jacob the Deceiver (Genesis 25:19-34; 27:1-41)	**21**
Rebekah, Woman of the Lord (25:19-34)	21
Papa's Boy and Mama's Boy	22
Obtaining the Birthright (25:29-34)	23
The Desire for Instant Gratification	24
Taking Shrewd Advantage (25:33)	24
Ethical Implications	24
Despising Spiritual Things (25:34)	25
Tricking Isaac into a Blessing (27:1-40)	26
Isaac Blesses Jacob (27:27-29)	28
What Kind of Blessing Is This?	29
Can God bless through Unrighteousness	30
God's sovereignty and man's free will	30
Preferring One Child over Another (25:28)	31
"Jacob Have I loved"	32

The High Cost of Favoritism (37:3-4)   94
Joseph's Dreams (37:5-11)   94
Selling Joseph into Slavery (37:12-36)   95
Joseph's Fortunes in Egypt (chapters 39-41)   96
A Famine Sends Jacob's Sons to Egypt (41:1-34)   97
Fear, Blame, and Stubbornness (42:35-38)   97
Preparing for the Second Trip to Egypt (43:1-13)   98
Jacob's Prayer (43:14)   99
Joseph Confronts His Brothers (43:15-44:34)   100
Joseph Makes Himself Known (45:1-24)   101
Jacob's Reassurance (45:25-46:27)   102
Jacob Journeys to Egypt (chapter 46)   103
And Joseph's Hand Will Close Your Eyes   104

7. Jacob Offers Blessings (Genesis 46:28-49:33)   **106**
Blessing   106
Blessing in the Bible   107
Joseph's Brothers Meet Pharaoh (46:31-47:12)   109
Jacob Blesses Pharaoh (47:7)   109
The Years of My Pilgrimage (47:8-9)   110
The Mindset of a Sojourner   110
Old Age in the Era of the Patriarchs   111
Extracting an Oath from Joseph (47:29-31)   112
Blessing Ephraim and Manasseh (48:1-20)   114
Prophetic Blessings   116
Blessing of Jacob's Twelve Sons (49:1-28)   117
Jacob Dies (49:33)   119
Difficult Years Have Brought Jacob to God   120
God Who Has Been My Shepherd   120
Do You Know the Shepherd?   121

Appendix - Participant Handouts   **123**

Table of Contents

Preface	3
Table of Contents	5
Reprint Guidelines	9
Online Bible Study Forum	10
References and Abbreviations	11
Introduction to Jacob's Life and Times	**12**
Jacob's Life in a Nutshell	12
Yahweh and the Religions of the Ancient Near East	13
The Patriarchs' Religion	14
Authorship of Genesis and the Pentateuch	15
Dating of Jacob	15
Chronology of Jacob	16
Chief Places Jacob Lived	18
1. Jacob the Deceiver (Genesis 25:19-34; 27:1-41)	**21**
Rebekah, Woman of the Lord (25:19-34)	21
Papa's Boy and Mama's Boy	22
Obtaining the Birthright (25:29-34)	23
The Desire for Instant Gratification	24
Taking Shrewd Advantage (25:33)	24
Ethical Implications	24
Despising Spiritual Things (25:34)	25
Tricking Isaac into a Blessing (27:1-40)	26
Isaac Blesses Jacob (27:27-29)	28
What Kind of Blessing Is This?	29
Can God bless through Unrighteousness	30
God's sovereignty and man's free will	30
Preferring One Child over Another (25:28)	31
"Jacob Have I loved"	32

    Conclusion   33

2. Jacob Meets God (Genesis 27:41-28:22)   34
    Esau's Grudge (27:41)   34
    Rebekah's Plan (27:42-45)   34
    Godly Marriage   35
    Religion of the Canaanites   35
    Polygamy in the Ancient Near East   36
    Jacob Is Sent Away to Find a Wife (27:46-28:2)   36
    The Blessing of Abraham (28:3-4)   37
    Jacob Begins His Journey (28:10-11)   39
    Jacob's Dream (28:11-12)   39
    God's Blessing in the Dream (28:13-15)   39
    Surely, the Lord Is in this Place (28:16-17)   41
    Jacob Sets Up a Stone to Yahweh (28:18a)   42
    Anointing the Stone (28:18b)   43
    Jacob's Holy Vow to Yahweh (28:20-22)   44
    The Promise to Return to Canaan (28:15b, 21a)   45
    Jacob Promises to Tithe (28:22)   45
    Tithing as Allegiance to a King   46
    Tithing as a Recognition of God's Supply   47

3. Jacob and Laban, Rachel and Leah (Genesis 29-31)   49
    Haran   49
    Jacob's Family in Haran   50
    Jacob the Servant (29:1-14)   50
    Love Is Blind (29:15-30)   51
    Jacob's Children (29:31-30:24)   53
    Jacob Negotiates with Laban (30:25-36)   55
    Breeding Variegated Sheep and Goats (30:37-43)   56
    God Commands Jacob to Return to Canaan (31:1-13)   57
    Rachel and Leah Back Jacob (31:14-16)   58
    Jacob's Family Escapes from Haran (31:17-21)   58
    Laban Pursues Jacob (31:22-30)   59
    Theft of Household Gods (31:30-35)   59
    The Covenant at Mizpah (31:36-55)   60
    Mizpah Is Not a Sentimental Word at Parting   62
    Blessing and Conflict   63

4. Jacob Wrestles with God and Man (Genesis 32-33) — 65
    Sign of the Angelic Army (32:1-2) — 65
    Preparing to Meet Esau (32:3-21) — 66
    1. Jacob sends messengers ahead — 66
    2. Jacob prays (32:9-12) — 67
    3. Jacob prepares a succession of gifts to appease Esau (32:13-21) — 69
    4. Jacob divides his party into two groups (32:7-8; 33:1-2) — 70
    Wrestling with God (32:22-32) — 70
    Unless You Bless Me (32:26) — 71
    A New Name: Israel (32:28) — 72
    Peniel – the Face of God (32:30) — 72
    Jacob's Limp (32:31-32) — 73
    Jacob Meets Esau (33:1-16) — 73
    Reflections on Jacob's Wrestling — 75
    Jesus Wrestled with His Father in the Garden — 76

5. Jacob Returns to Bethel (Genesis 33:17-35:29) — 78
    Living in Succoth (33:17) — 78
    Jacob Settles in Shechem (33:18-20) — 78
    The Rape of Dinah (34:1-5) — 79
    Jacob's Sons Deceive Shechem (34:6-24) — 79
    Jacob Intervenes – Too Late (34:30-31) — 80
    The Dangers of Intermarriage — 81
    The Time to Teach a Nation — 83
    Intermarriage in the New Testament — 83
    If You Are Married to an Unbelieving Spouse — 83
    A Call to Rededication (35:1-15) — 84
    Washing Bodies and Clothes (35:2) — 85
    The Washing of Repentance — 86
    Building the Altar at Bethel (35:6-7) — 87
    God Appears to Jacob Again (35:9-13) — 87
    Acts of Worship (35:14-15) — 88
    A Forgotten Vow? — 89
    Four Heartaches — 90
    Talking with God — 92

6. Jacob's Depression, Fear, and Hope (Genesis 37-47) — 93
    The Loss of Joseph (chapter 37) — 93

The High Cost of Favoritism (37:3-4)   94
Joseph's Dreams (37:5-11)   94
Selling Joseph into Slavery (37:12-36)   95
Joseph's Fortunes in Egypt (chapters 39-41)   96
A Famine Sends Jacob's Sons to Egypt (41:1-34)   97
Fear, Blame, and Stubbornness (42:35-38)   97
Preparing for the Second Trip to Egypt (43:1-13)   98
Jacob's Prayer (43:14)   99
Joseph Confronts His Brothers (43:15-44:34)   100
Joseph Makes Himself Known (45:1-24)   101
Jacob's Reassurance (45:25-46:27)   102
Jacob Journeys to Egypt (chapter 46)   103
And Joseph's Hand Will Close Your Eyes   104

7. Jacob Offers Blessings (Genesis 46:28-49:33)   **106**

Blessing   106
Blessing in the Bible   107
Joseph's Brothers Meet Pharaoh (46:31-47:12)   109
Jacob Blesses Pharaoh (47:7)   109
The Years of My Pilgrimage (47:8-9)   110
The Mindset of a Sojourner   110
Old Age in the Era of the Patriarchs   111
Extracting an Oath from Joseph (47:29-31)   112
Blessing Ephraim and Manasseh (48:1-20)   114
Prophetic Blessings   116
Blessing of Jacob's Twelve Sons (49:1-28)   117
Jacob Dies (49:33)   119
Difficult Years Have Brought Jacob to God   120
God Who Has Been My Shepherd   120
Do You Know the Shepherd?   121

Appendix - Participant Handouts   **123**

Reprint Guidelines

You are free to print out a copy of this book for your own use in this study.

Copying the Handouts. In some cases, small groups or Sunday school classes would like to use these notes to study this material. That's great. An appendix provides copies of handouts designed for classes and small groups. There is no charge whatsoever to print out as many copies of the handouts as you need for participants.

All charts and notes are copyrighted and must bear the line: "Copyright © 2010, Ralph F. Wilson. All rights reserved. Reprinted by permission."

You may not resell these notes to other groups or individuals outside your congregation. You may, however, charge people in your group enough to cover your copying costs.

Copying the book (or the majority of it) in your congregation or group, you are requested to purchase a reprint license for each book. A Reprint License, $2.50 for each copy is available for purchase at

www.jesuswalk.com/books/jacob.htm

Or you may send a check to:

    Dr. Ralph F. Wilson
    JesusWalk Publications
    PO Box 565
    Loomis, CA 95650, USA

The Scripture says,

"The laborer is worthy of his hire" (Luke 10:7) and "Anyone who receives instruction in the word must share all good things with his instructor" (Galatians 6:6).

However, if you are from a third world country or an area where it is difficult to transmit money, please make a small contribution instead to help the poor in your community.

Online Bible Study Forum

Each chapter in this study contains four or five questions to help you learn and process what you've been studying. As you engage your mind in the attempt to frame an answer, you'll begin to understand the issues raised in the Scripture text and the implications of applying the principles in your own life.

But learning is better with others. This book began as an interactive e-mail Bible study. One component of this learning approach has been to give students a chance to post their answers to the questions in an online Forum and read how others answered the questions as a way of deepening learning. You'll find that each of the questions in the chapters contains a web address where you, too, can take advantage of the Forum.

However, if you want to participate in the Forum, you'll need to agree to some basic guidelines (www.jesuswalk.com/admin/pu_forum_guidelines.htm). In short:

- No denomination or religion bashing.
- Practice a loving spirit.
- Comments may be removed in the future.
- Stay on topic.
- Be discrete. Don't give out your e-mail address or share things too personal.

If you haven't participated in the Forum before, you'll need to register first. To keep from getting confused, why don't you Read the Instructions for the Forum. They will explain exactly how to register (www.joyfulheart.com/forums/instructions.htm).

Once you've registered for the Forum you can introduce yourself to others in this study (www.joyfulheart.com/forums/index.php?showtopic=922) and get started with the questions posed in each chapter.

References and Abbreviations

BDB	Francis Brown, S.R. Driver, and Charles A. Briggs, *A Hebrew and English Lexicon of the Old Testament* (Clarendon Press: Oxford, originally published 1907, reprinted with corrections 1953). ISBN 0198643012.
DOTP	T. Desmond Alexander and David W. Baker, *Dictionary of the Old Testament: Pentateuch* (InterVarsity Press, 2003). ISBN 0830817816.
Hamilton	Victor P. Hamilton, *The Book of Genesis, Chapters 1-17* (New International Commentary on the Old Testament; Eerdmans, 1990) and Victor P. Hamilton, *The Book of Genesis, Chapters 18-50* (New International Commentary on the Old Testament; Eerdmans, 1995). ISBNs 0802823084 and 0802823092.
Holladay	William L. Holladay, *A Concise Hebrew and Aramaic Lexicon of the Old Testament* based on the Lexical work of Ludwig Koehler and Walter Baumbartner (Grand Rapids: Eerdmans / Leiden: E. J. Brill, 1988). ISBN 0802834132.
ISBE	Geoffrey W. Bromiley (general editor), *The International Standard Bible Encyclopedia* (Eerdmans, 1979-1988; fully revised from the 1915 edition). ISBN 0802837859.
Kidner	Derek Kidner, *Genesis* (Tyndale Old Testament Commentaries; InterVarsity Press, 1968). ISBN 0877842515.
KJV	*King James Version* (Authorized Version, 1611)
NIV	*New International Version* (International Bible Society, 1973, 1978)
NRSV	*New Revised Standard Version* (Division of Christian Education of the National Council of Churches of Christ USA, 1989)
TWOT	R. Laird Harris, Gleason L. Archer, Jr., and Bruce K. Waltke, editors), *Theological Wordbook of the Old Testament* (2 volumes, Moody Press, 1980). ISBN 0802486312.

Introduction to Jacob's Life and Times

As we begin our study of the life of Jacob, we'll be traveling back through time nearly 4,000 years into a semi-nomadic, Middle Bronze Age culture far removed from our own. While many of the customs will be explained in the lessons to follow, here's an introduction to Jacob's life and times. (Note: Unless otherwise designated, all scripture references are to Genesis.)

James J. Tissot, "Isaac Sends Esau to Hunt" (c. 1896-1902), gouache on board, Jewish Museum, New York.

Jacob's Life in a Nutshell

You can't adequately sum up Jacob's career in just a few paragraphs, but for the sake of perspective, here's an attempt:

Jacob is the grandson of Abraham, to whom God revealed himself, and the son of Isaac. He is born a twin and spends his life in sibling rivalry with his (slightly) older brother Esau.

He has two streaks that will dominate his life: a sly, deceptive nature and a quest for spiritual things. As his spiritual side grows, his deceptive side diminishes.

Because his deceptive behavior incurs Esau's anger, Jacob flees for his life to Haran, the family's ancestral home in Mesopotamia. There he acquires two wives, two concubines, and a dozen children. When he arrives in Haran, he has only the clothes on his back to call his own. He leaves 20 years later a man of wealth, which he attributes to God's blessing.

As he returns to Canaan, he wrestles with God, reconciles with Esau, and settles again in the Promised Land, where he lives at Succoth, Shechem, Bethel, Hebron, and finally Goshen in Egypt. His sons are jealous of his favorite son Joseph, whom they sell into slavery. But Joseph eventually rises to second in command of all Egypt.

When Jacob is an old man, a famine devastates Canaan, forcing the family to buy grain in Egypt. Through a course of events, Joseph reconciles with his brothers and moves the entire clan to Egypt, where Jacob dies at the age of 147.

There it is in a nutshell, but we'll spend seven weeks examining the lessons and significance of his life.

Stele of Ur-Nammu (ca. 2200 BC), detail showing the crescent moon, the moon god's symbol.

Yahweh and the Religions of the Ancient Near East

Jacob grows up with the monotheistic faith of his father and grandfather, but the members of the family in Mesopotamia are idolaters and polytheists, worshippers of many gods (Joshua 24:2).

Jacob's wife Rachel, who grows up in Mesopotamia, steals her father's "household gods" (31:32-35; 35:2-4). Her family's names – Terah, Laban, Sarah, and Milcah – contain linguistic elements that reveal allegiance to the moon-god,[1] who is referred to in several inscriptions as "Sin/Shahar, the Lord of Haran."[2] He was the tutelary god of Haran.

Worship of the moon god involved temples as well as ziggurats with small temples on the top. These temples were staffed by priests (who offered sacrifices and made

---

[1] Kidner, *Genesis*, p. 111. Sarai (Sarah) is the equivalent of *sarratu*, "queen," an Akkadian translation of a Sumerian name for Ningal, the female partner of the moon-god Sin. Milcah is the same as the name of the goddess Malkatu, the daughter of Sin. Laban means "white," or "white one," a poetic name for the full moon (Hamilton, *Genesis 1-17*, p. 363).

[2] Alfred J. Hoerth, Gerald L. Mattingly, and Edwin M. Yamauchi, *Peoples of the Old Testament World* (Baker Book House/Lutterworth Press, 1994), p. 226.

libations), singers and musicians, as well as male and female prostitutes (whose activities many scholars relate to the fertility cult).[3] Much later than Jacob, the Israelites are warned against worship of the moon, sun, and stars (Deuteronomy 4:19; 17:2-5), though this kind of worship continued under idolatrous kings (2 Kings 23:5-12).

The Patriarchs' Religion

Jacob, however, is a monotheist, a worshipper of one God. He uses primarily three words for God.

1. *El* is the generic Canaanite name for the cosmic deity.

2. *Yahweh* is God's revealed name. It is sometimes translated "Jehovah" in the KJV, but usually it is expressed as "LORD" in English Bibles, following the Jewish tradition of not pronouncing the divine name, but substituting *Adonai*, "Lord," instead.[4]

3. *El Shaddai* ("Almighty God") is used occasionally by Isaac and Jacob (28:3; 35:11; 43:14; 48:3; 49:25).

The monotheism of the patriarchs contrasts sharply with the polytheism of their forebears (Joshua 24:2). The patriarchs believe God to be the Lord of the cosmos (14:22; 24:3), supreme judge of mankind (15:14;18:25), controller of nature (18:14; 19:24; 20:17), highly exalted (14:22) and eternal (21:33).[5]

Their relationship with God is personal rather than formal. However, Jacob and the other patriarchs practiced various forms of worship, including building altars, erecting stones, offering sacrifices and libations, calling on the name of Yahweh, circumcision, prayer, making vows, and tithing. We'll examine some of these further as we study the details of Jacob's life.

---

[3] Robert H. Stein, "Sumer," ISBE 4:653-662.

[4] It may appear in Exodus 3:8 that God had never before been called Yahweh, but that clearly isn't the case. The revelation of I AM to Moses was new, but Yahweh had been worshipped by Abraham and his descendents and had found its way into the names of their children for generations. "In Exodus 6:3 the Lord explains to Moses that by his name Yahweh he had not been "known" to the patriarchs, meaning "know" (see *yada'*) in its fullest sense: the name was in use (12:8; 15:2, 7, 8) but was not appreciated in the redemptive significance that it acquired under Moses. (J. A. Motyer, *The Revelation of the Divine Name*, cited in TWOT #484).

[5] Roland K. Harrison, "Abraham," ISBE 1:17.

Authorship of Genesis and the Pentateuch

Though the traditional view is that Moses was the author of the Pentateuch, there has been growing speculation about authorship since the Enlightenment. The most celebrated and complex theory of authorship was advanced by German Old Testament scholar Julius Wellhausen (1844-1918), referred to as "the Documentary Hypothesis." He theorized four sources which are abbreviated JEDP:

- J   Yahwistic
- E   Eloistic
- D   Deuteronomic
- P   Priestly

The Yahwistic strand could be identified, so goes the theory, by the editor's use of Yahweh (Jehovah) or LORD for God; the Eloistic strand by the use of El for God. Wellhausen was widely influential and the theory grew more and more complex – and speculative. These days, however, Wellhausen's JEDP theory is in disarray. R.N. Whybray commented in 1995 on the state of Pentateuchal studies:

> "There is at the present moment no consensus whatever about when, why, how, and through whom the Pentateuch reached its present form, and opinions about the dates of composition of its various parts differ by more than five hundred years."[6]

Certainly Jesus, the Jews, and the early church all believed that the Pentateuch (which the Jews referred to as "the law") was inspired by God and attributed it as a whole to Moses. It is likely that the materials Moses and other early editors worked with represent oral and written traditions dated much earlier than themselves. Whether Moses was the first to write down the stories of Abraham and his descendents, or served as an editor himself, we just don't know.[7]

Our focus will not be on speculative theories of sources, but on the Book of Genesis that comes down to us in the Bible and the meaning of that revelation.

Dating of Jacob

When did Jacob live? Dating is complex. It is difficult to find fixed events in Genesis that can be connected absolutely to dates established from archaeology.

---

[6] R.N. Whybray, *Introduction to the Pentateuch* (Eerdmans, 1995), pp. 12-13, cited in T. Desmond Alexander, "Authorship of the Pentateuch," DOTP 61-72.

[7] Alexander, DOTP 61-72; Hamilton, *Genesis* 1-17, pp. 11-38.

One approach to dating the patriarchs is to backtrack from the first fixed event we find in the Bible – a statement that Solomon laid the temple foundation in the 480th year after the exodus (1 Kings 6:1), which would date the exodus at about 1447-1446 BC. This is the so-called "early dating." Working backward from the genealogies and other data in the Pentateuch puts the birth of Jacob's grandfather Abraham in 2166 BC.[8]

Another approach to dating uses a combination of history and archaeology. There are no archaeological findings that refer specifically to Abraham, Isaac, and Jacob, so where they fit into the archaeological periods is not precise.[9]

Chronology of Jacob

An early date for the Exodus would put the birth of Jacob and Esau at about 2006 BC,[10] while a late date for the Exodus puts the birth year around 1835 BC.[11] As I've

---

[8] Eugene H. Merrill, "Chronology," DOTP 121, Table 3. There are problems, however. First, textual: the Greek Septuagint and the Samaritan Pentateuch agree with Paul (Galatians 3:17) that the 430 years of Exodus 12:40 apply to the whole time span between Abraham and the Exodus, not just the Israelite stay in Egypt as the Hebrew Masoretic text would suggest, bringing Abraham's birth year to 1952 BC (John N. Oswalt, "Chronology of the OT," ISBE 1:673-685). Second, genealogies in the Bible occasionally skip generations.

[9] One prong is the dating of the destruction of Sodom and Gomorrah (Genesis 19) by some kind of cataclysmic event, which archaeological evidence seems to point to around 1900 BC (Roland K. Harrison, "Cities of the Valley," ISBE 1:704; Roland K. Harrison, "Abraham," ISBE 1:17). You can also compare the lifestyle described in Genesis to archaeological findings to find a match. At the end of the Early Bronze Age (2400 to 2000 BC), Palestine was in a pre-urban phase, with numerous settlements, camps, and cemeteries in the Jordan Valley and the Negev-Sinai. The Palestine described in Genesis also was sparsely populated, with few if any urban centers. By about 1800 BC, a number of urban centers had developed -- Dan, Hazor, Akko, Shechem, Aphek, Jerusalem, Jericho, and Ashdod. By 1600 BC, there were a number of heavily fortified sites, such as Gezer and Shechem. But, by 1550 BC, nearly every city in Palestine had been destroyed by the Egyptians driving out the Hyksos from Egypt (Mark W. Chavalas, "Archaeology," DOTP 37-49. John Arthur Thompson, "Shechem," DBA, 410-411). The Hyksos, a Semitic rather than Egyptian people, ruled over Syria, Palestine, and Egypt from 1650 to 1542 BC until they were driven out by the Egyptian Amosis (Pharaoh Amenhotep I), founder of the Eighteenth Dynasty. It is easier to image the non-Egyptian slave Joseph rising to the position of second in the kingdom under a Hyksos ruler (1786 to 1575 BC), than under an Egyptian ruler, either before or after the Hyksos period. The period after the Hyksos dynasties would be expected to yield the pharaoh "who knew not Joseph" (Exodus 1:8), who would oppress the Semitic peoples remaining in Egypt (Hamilton, *Genesis* 1:59-67.) Depending upon how one views the evidence, Abraham might fit into Middle Bronze I (2100-1900 BC, Nelson Glueck and William F. Albright), Middle Bronze II (1900-1550, Ephraim A. Speiser), or the Amarna Period of the Late Bronze Age (early 14th century, Cyrus H. Gordon). Barry J. Beitzel (*The Moody Atlas of Bible Lands* (Moody Press, 1985), pp. 82-86) sees the patriarchal sojourn in Canaan from 1875 to 1660 BC, with Joseph promoted about 1670 BC, in the middle of the Hyksos occupation of Egypt.

Introduction to Jacob's Life and Times

studied the issues, the early date for the Exodus makes more sense to me. The following dates are based on an early date for the Exodus.[12]

2006 BC	Birth of Jacob and Esau, probably in Beer-lahai-roi	25:26
1966	Marriage of Esau in Beersheba, age 40	26:34
1930	Jacob's journey to Haran, age 76	28:2
1923	Jacob's marriages, age 83, Haran	29:23, 28
1918	Birth of Judah, Jacob's age 88	29:35
1916	End of Jacob's 14 year labor for his wives, Jacob's age 90	29:30
1916	Birth of Joseph	30:23
1910	End of Jacob's stay with Laban, age 96	31:41
1910	Jacob's arrival at Shechem	33:18
1902	Rape of Dinah	34:1-2
1900	Marriage of Judah, Judah is 18, Jacob is 106	38:1-2
1899	Selling of Joseph, Joseph is 17, Jacob is 107	37:2, 27
1888	Joseph imprisoned	39:20; cf. 41:1
1886	Joseph released from prison, made ruler of Egypt	41:1, 46
1886	Death of Isaac, Isaac is 180, Jacob is 120	35:28
1879	Beginning of famine, Jacob is 127	41:54
1878	Brothers' first visit to Egypt	42:1-2
1877	Brothers' second visit to Egypt	43:1; 45:6, 11
1876	Jacob's descent to Egypt at age 130	46:6; cf. 47:9
1859	Death of Jacob at age 147	47:28
1806	Death of Joseph at age 110	50:22

---

[10] An early date for the Exodus is based primarily on 1 Kings 6:1. For a detailed discussion of Old Testament chronology and how archeological finds bear on the issue see John N. Oswalt, "Chronology of the OT," ISBE 1:673-685; John H. Walton, "Exodus, Date of," DOTP, pp. 258-272.

[11] A late date for the Exodus is based primarily on the reconstructions of archeologists.

[12] Based primarily on Eugene H. Merrill, "Chronology," DOTP, p. 121, Table 3: Patriarchal Chronological Data.

Chief Places Jacob Lived

As a semi-nomadic shepherd, Jacob moved frequently, especially in his earlier years. Here are some of the places he lived.

Beer-lahai-roi

Beer-lahai-roi, Jacob's birthplace (25:11) means, "well of the Living One who sees me" (16:7). It is the site of a well in the Negev desert south of Beersheba, on the road to Shur, between Kadesh and Bered (16:14).[13]

Beersheba

Beersheba, where Jacob lived as a boy, was the site of another well in the northern Negev desert. The name means "well of seven." It contains rich alluvial soil where crops could be grown and herds could be grazed. The region was controlled by Gerar, the nearest commercial center.[14]

Gerar

Gerar was a town in the western Negev desert, near Gaza, apparently controlled by Philistine or sea tribes during the patriarchal period (26:1, 8). Isaac and Jacob spent some time in Gerar (26:1) during their desert wanderings.[15]

Haran

Haran, where Jacob labored for 20 years and raised his family, was the ancestral homeland of Jacob's ancestors. It is in present-day Turkey along the Jullab River.[16]

---

[13] According to Arab tradition, it may possibly be identified with modern 'Ain Muweileh, about 7 miles west of Kadesh-barnea and about 47 miles southwest of Beer-sheba (D.D. Gerard, "Beer-Lahai-Roi," ISBE 1:448).

[14] Tell es-Seba', the site of the ancient town, is located at the juncture of the Wadi Seba' and the Wadi Khelil (Anson F. Rainey, "Beer-sheba," ISBE 1:448-451).

[15] Gerar has been tentatively identified with Tell Abu Hureirah (Anson F. Rainey, "Gerar," ISBE 2:446-447).

[16] Haran lies along the Jullab River, near the source of the Balikh River, 24 miles southeast of the Turkish city Urfa, and 60 miles north of the confluence of the Euphrates and Balikh Rivers. It is located on the main road that ran from Nineveh to Carchemish and was regarded as of considerable importance by the Assyrian kings. Its chief cult was that of the Mesopotamian moon-god Sin. It was probably founded as a merchant outpost by the Sumerian city of Ur in the late third millennium BC. The name Haran means "highway, road, or caravan" in Akkadian. Today a village on this site consists of beehive shaped houses. Archaeological evidence includes inscriptional evidence for the Sin temple (from the beginning of the second millennium), a stella of the moon-god, and violent destruction about 610 BC by the Scythians,

Succoth

Succoth, near where the Jabbok River enters the Jordan, was named after the booths (*sukkâ*) that Jacob built there for his livestock after reconciling with Easu and returning to Canaan (33:17).[17]

Shechem

Shechem is an ancient walled city that guarded the pass between Mount Ebal and Mount Gerizim, on the main road from Jerusalem to the north. Jacob's family camped on land outside the city near the Tree of Moreh (33:18).[18]

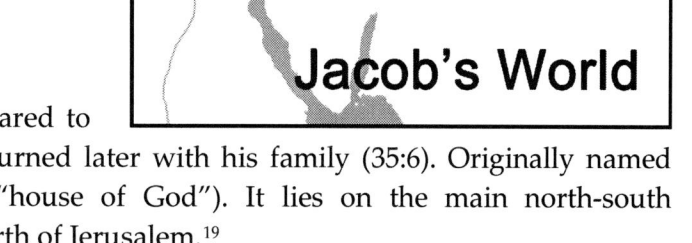

Bethel

Bethel is where God first appeared to Jacob (28:10-22) and where he returned later with his family (35:6). Originally named Luz, Jacob renamed it Beth-el ("house of God"). It lies on the main north-south watershed route about 12 miles north of Jerusalem.[19]

Hebron

Hebron (meaning "league" or "confederacy"), lies about 19 miles south of Jerusalem, close to the Tree of Mamre. It was an occasional home for Jacob (37:14) and the final residence of Isaac (35:27). At Sarah's death, Abraham had purchased a burial cave at

---

Medes, and Chaldeans (Mark W. Chavalas, "Haran," DOTP 379-381; Robert J. Hughes, III, "Haran," ISBE 2:614).

[17] It is located in the territory assigned to the tribe of Gad (Joshua 13:27) near the Jordan Valley, usually identified with Tell Deir 'Alla, two miles north of the Jabbok River (R.D. Patterson, "*sākak*, TWOT #1492e).

[18] Shechem was a city-state founded about 1900 BC, in the Amorite period of the Middle Bronze IIA era. It is referred to in Egyptian inscriptions both of conquered cities and among Asiatic enemies of Egypt (G. Ernest Wright and E.F. Campbell, "Shechem," ISBE 4:458-462).

[19] Luz was founded about 2000 BC. In the early Hyksos period (about 1750 BC) the city wall on the north side was reinforced with a wide clay revetment (William Ewing and Roland K. Harrison, "Bethel," ISBE 1:465-467).

nearby Machpelah from Ephron the Hittite (23:1-20). Abraham, Isaac, and Jacob and other family members were buried there (35:27-29; 47:30; 49:30; 50:13).[20]

Goshen

Goshen is a district in Egypt where Jacob lived the last 18 years of his life. The Israelites lived here until the Exodus centuries later in an area known as the "district of Ramases" (47:6, 11), probably near Pi-Ramases.[21]

We've placed Jacob and his family in history and in geography. Now it's time to examine their story to see what we can learn about their God – and ours.

---

[20] Numbers 32:22 indicates that Hebron was built seven years before the Egyptian city of Zoan (Tanis), probably a Hyksos building project, dating it at approximately 1700 BC, though it had probably been inhabited since the Early Bronze period onward. The traditional site of the cave of Machpelah is now marked by a mosque, formerly a Crusader church. Little archaeological excavation has been done there. ("Negev," *Archeological Encyclopedia of the Holy Land*, pp. 171-172; John J. Davis, "Hebron," DAT 232-233.

[21] Its exact location is uncertain, depending upon the location of the Hyksos dynasty capital of Avaris or Tanis. Goshen was probably located near Pi-Ramses. The name "Goshen" is found in the name Phacusa (modern Faqus). According to the narrative of Abbess Astheria, Faqus is only four miles from Pi-Ramses (thus locating it), which places Goshen close to the Egyptian seat of government. (Harold G. Stigers, "*gōshen*, TWOT #390).

1. Jacob the Deceiver (Genesis 25:19-34; 27:1-41)

We've entered an era that seems so very far removed from the twenty-first century. How can shepherds and nomads living in goatskin tents in the arid climes of the Middle East four millennia ago have any relevance to us? Once we understand the culture a bit, we find that people haven't changed that much in three or four millennia. The special factor, however, is God, who reveals himself to these ancients. He is the One we seek to learn about, the One we seek to know.

James J. Tissot, "The Mess of Pottage" (c. 1896-1902), gouache on board, 21.3 x 26.8 cm, Jewish Museum, New York.

Rebekah, Woman of the Lord (25:19-34)

"¹⁹ This is the account of Abraham's son Isaac. Abraham became the father of Isaac, ²⁰ and Isaac was forty years old when he married Rebekah daughter of Bethuel the Aramean from Paddan Aram and sister of Laban the Aramean." (25:19-20)

Abraham – patriarch of what will become Israel – has one legitimate son, Isaac. This son has married his cousin, Rebekah, who moves from far-away Haran (near the border between Turkey and Iraq), to Canaan.

Rebekah feels isolated in this new land – and is shamefully barren. It is shameful because for a women to be childless in that culture is to be incapable of performing her primary function – bearing children. Failure to produce an heir is a major calamity for the family in the ancient Near East.

She has a husband who loves her – that is something! (24:66). And her husband prays for her.

> "Isaac prayed to the LORD on behalf of his wife, because she was barren. The LORD answered his prayer, and his wife Rebekah became pregnant." (25:21)

The Lord answers his prayer – twice over. Rebekah is pregnant with twins!

> "²² The babies jostled each other within her, and she said, 'Why is this happening to me?' So she went to inquire of the LORD. ²³ The LORD said to her,
>
>> 'Two nations are in your womb,
>> and two peoples from within you will be separated;
>> one people will be stronger than the other,
>> and the older will serve the younger.'" (25:21b-23)

Rebecca has heard from the Lord. She is a spiritual woman.

Papa's Boy and Mama's Boy

> "²⁴ When the time came for her to give birth, there were twin boys in her womb. ²⁵ The first to come out was red, and his whole body was like a hairy garment; so they named him Esau. ²⁶ After this, his brother came out, with his hand grasping Esau's heel; so he was named Jacob. Isaac was sixty years old when Rebekah gave birth to them." (25:24-26)

The birth itself is an acted prophecy of the future. Esau comes out first, red and hairy.[1] Jacob follows his brother straightaway. His tiny hand grips[2] his brother's heel (*'āqēb*) as they pull Esau out, and they have to pry his little fingers off to free Esau. Jacob is born second, but he is grasping to be first from the earliest moments of his life. They name him Jacob (*ya'aqōb*), which means, "he grasps the heel," or figuratively, "he deceives."[3]

Isaac is sixty when the boys are born. Rebekah is in her early to mid-thirties by this time. The boys bring great joy into Isaac's life, especially his firstborn. Esau loves the out-of-doors[4] like his dad and they would go hunting together. The boy becomes a

---

[1] Esau (*'ēśāw*) faintly resembles the word "hairy" (*śē'ār*), but Esau's future homeland is called Seir (*śē'îr*) as well as Edom ("red"), perhaps after the red sandstone characteristic of the area. (Robin J. DeWitt Knauth, "Esau, Edomites," DOTP 219-224).

[2] *'Āḥaz*, "grasp, take hold, take possession" (BDB 28).

[3] The verb *'āqab* means "take by the heel, supplant," related to the noun *'āqēb*, "heel" (J. Barton Payne, *'āqab*, TWOT #1676f).

[4] *Śādeh*, "field, country, ground, land." *This* masculine noun broadly designates the open field, country, or a definite portion of ground, a field (TWOT #2236).

1. Jacob the Deceiver (Genesis 25:19-34; 27:1-41)

skilled[5], renowned hunter, who tracks deer in the wilderness and brings them down with his bow and arrow. Esau is happiest when he is out hunting in the wild (25:27a).

Jacob is just the opposite. He is quieter[6] and stays around the tents (25:27b). He and his mother Rebekah grow close, and she helps him understand something of his destiny. No doubt, she tells him of the prophecy that he will rule over his brother. She implants the idea, reinforces it, and – as we'll see – pushes him to fulfill it.

Obtaining the Birthright (25:29-34)

One day while Esau is out hunting, Jacob is at home cooking lentil[7] stew[8] in a pot over the fire. (The KJV calls it "pottage."[9]). Esau is exhausted and famished. He craves the red-colored stew. "Quick, let me have some of that red stew!" He can't wait. This is Jacob's opportunity.

"First, sell[10] me your birthright," he says. The "birthright" or "primogeniture" (*bekōrâ*) involved the legal rights of the firstborn to a double portion of the inheritance (Deuteronomy 21:17), plus leadership of the family or clan when the father died. Esau, the firstborn, is destined to rule over Jacob all his life – unless he is foolish enough to part with his legal rights.

"Hey, I'm about to die," replies Esau. "What good is the birthright to me?"

This exchange tells us a great deal about the character of both brothers.

---

[5] "Skillful" (NIV, NRSV), "cunning" (KJV) is *yāda'*, "to know." The participle occurs in phrases describing skill in hunting (Genesis 25:27), learning (Isaiah 29:11-13), lamentation (Amos 5:16), sailing the sea (2 Chronicles 8:18), and playing an instrument (1 Samuel 16:16) (TWOT #848).

[6] "Quiet" (NIV, NRSV), "plain" (KJV) is *tām*, "Perfect," so translated in nine of thirteen occurrences, many of which refer to the patriarch Job. It also means "undefiled, upright," from *tāmam*, "be complete" (TWOT #2522c). Kidner (p. 152) sees a suggestion of "sound" or "solid," "the level-headed quality that made Jacob, at his best, toughly dependable, and at his worst a formidably cool opponent." Hamilton (pp. 181-182) surveys the possibilities and settles on the translation of "wholesome man."

[7] In Genesis 25:34 this is called "lentil stew" (*'adāshîm*). The lentil (also known as daal or dal, *Lens culinaris*), a type of pulse, is a bushy annual plant of the legume family, grown for its lens-shaped seeds. It is about 15 inches tall and the seeds grow in pods, usually with two seeds in each.

[8] "Cooking" (NIV), "sod" (KJV, obsolete past tense of "seethe," that is, "boil") is the verb *zîd*, "boil" (TWOT #547). The related word, "stew" (NIV, NRSV), "pottage" (KJV) *nāzîd*, "boiled food, pottage," from *zîd*, "boil" (TWOT #547d).

[9] In English, "pottage" is "a thick soup of vegetables and often meat," from "pot." The phrase "mess of pottage" isn't in the Bible, but comes from a section heading in the Geneva Bible (1560). "Mess" is an archaic usage meaning "food set on a table at one time," preserved in our word "mess hall."

[10] "Sell" is *mākar*, used for all kinds of sales, including selling into slavery. The Nuzi tablets (c. 1500 BC) witness two other cases of men yielding inheritance rights to a younger brother for some immediate temporal consideration (TWOT #1194).

The Desire for Instant Gratification

Esau betrays his own tendency towards instant gratification. "I want it now. I can't wait for the future." In so doing, he bargains away his future options. Jacob, on the other hand, is willing to deny himself in the present to obtain in the future what he values most. Each of us faces temptations – strong temptations – to get our gratification now. We want instant pleasure, instant wealth, instant popularity. And for this we trade away our futures. Jacob is an example of a person who can live with delayed gratification.

Taking Shrewd Advantage (25:33)

Jacob's motives aren't pure, of course. Esau accuses him of deceiving (27:36), though Jacob isn't guilty of deception – this time. Instead, Jacob takes advantage of Esau's weakness. In a weak moment he extracts from his brother a binding promise.

> "'Swear[11] to me first.' So he swore an oath to him, selling his birthright to Jacob." (25:33)

Could such an inherent right as a birthright be sold or transferred in this manner? There's no clear precedent, either in ancient literature or Biblical literature. There is a 15th Century BC text from Nuzi as a parallel where a man named Tupkitilla transfers his inheritance rights to a grove over to his brother Kurpazah in exchange for three sheep. While not parallel in every aspect, it does indicate that one brother could sell inherited property to another.[12] In Ruth 4 we see a legal transaction between Boaz and his relative which gives Boaz the right to marry Ruth – and purchase her mother-in-law Naomi's property. The relative relinquishes his right and formalizes it by taking off his sandal and giving it to Boaz in the presence of witnesses.

Though Esau sells his birthright on the spur of the moment in a casual setting, it seems to have been considered binding. Neither Esau nor Isaac seem to question that Jacob has indeed obtained the birthright (25:34; 27:35-36).

Ethical Implications

Is Jacob being honest? Is he being a good businessman? Do we really get ahead by taking advantage of others' weaknesses and shortsightedness? Are we obligated to disclose to others their potential mistakes? How can we love our neighbor as ourselves in business?

---

[11] "Swear" is *shāba'*, "swear, adjure, bind oneself by an oath" (TWOT #2319).
[12] Discussed by Hamilton, *Genesis*, pp. 183-184.

Jay Conrad Levinson wrote a whole series of books beginning with *Guerrilla Marketing* (1984), based on the hypothesis that business is war and conflict, and that the little guy can gain advantage by being smarter, quick on his feet – and ruthless.

I think Jesus calls us to a higher standard in our business practices. He would be much more pleased by the "win-win" deal, than the one that took advantage of the weakness of a brother. His "Golden Rule" is: "Do to others as you would have them do to you" (Luke 6:31). Jacob doesn't love his brother as himself.

Despising Spiritual Things (25:34)

> "Then Jacob gave Esau some bread and some lentil stew. He ate and drank, and then got up and left. So Esau despised his birthright." (25:34)

This incident also says a lot about one's value of spiritual things, if we can consider the birthright in a spiritual as well as legal light. Esau values stew more than the birthright, while Jacob values the birthright more than his own integrity. The narrator notes, "So Esau despised his birthright" (25:34). "Despised" is *bāzâ*, "to despise, distain, hold in contempt," with the root meaning, "to accord little worth to something."[13]

The author of Hebrews discusses this incident:

> "See that no one ... is godless like Esau, who for a single meal sold his inheritance rights as the oldest son. Afterward, as you know, when he wanted to inherit this blessing, he was rejected. He could bring about no change of mind, though he sought the blessing with tears." (Hebrews 12:15-17)

Indeed, Esau *did* seek his father's blessing with tears:

> "When Esau heard his father's words, he burst out with a loud and bitter cry and said to his father, 'Bless me – me too, my father!'" (27:34)

> "'Do you have only one blessing, my father? Bless me too, my father!' Then Esau wept aloud." (27:38)

God is merciful and can forgive us of sin, but there are some doors we forever close for ourselves by our actions, actions that cannot be undone. This is for us a sobering warning, which speaks directly to our character and what we value most.

---

[13] Bruce K. Waltke, *bāzâ*, TWOT #224.

> Q1. Why does the New Testament condemn Esau for selling his birthright? (Hebrews 12:16-17) What did selling the birthright represent? What does this transaction say about Esau's character and values? What does it reveal about Jacob's character and values?
> http://www.joyfulheart.com/forums/index.php?showtopic=923

> Q2. Was Rebekah a spiritual woman, that is, interested in spiritual things? Was Isaac a spiritual man? Which do you think was the more spiritually sensitive? What evidence of spirituality do you see in Jacob? In Esau?
> http://www.joyfulheart.com/forums/index.php?showtopic=924

Tricking Isaac into a Blessing (27:1-40)

While Jacob's acquisition of the birthright might have been strictly legal, his acquisition of his father's blessing is grossly deceptive and unrighteous on its very face.

Genesis 27:1-40 contains the fascinating but dark story of conspiracy and fraud. Pause now and read it from your Bible.

Isaac is now about 135 years old, bedridden and nearly blind. Tent walls are thin. Jacob's mother Rebekah overhears Isaac telling Esau to hunt some venison and cook it for him, and then receive the formal father-to-son blessing of the firstborn before Isaac dies.

1. Jacob the Deceiver (Genesis 25:19-34; 27:1-41)

Rebekah remembers – though Isaac doesn't seem to – that this is all wrong. The Lord had told her "the older will serve the younger" (25:23).

Now Rebekah takes it upon herself to make the prophecy happen. She decides that Isaac must not bless Esau. You could argue that Rebekah is more spiritual than her husband Isaac, in that she remembers God's word and makes sure that nothing – not even righteousness and her husband's will – will stand in the way of God's will for her favorite son, Jacob. Call it what you will, what she proposes is pure deceit.

Quickly, Rebekah calls her favorite son Jacob. Do what I say, she says. Trick your father into giving you his blessing rather than Esau. She comes up with a scheme to trick the old man:

James J. Tissot, "Jacob Deceives Isaac" (c. 1896-1902), gouache on board, 16.9 x 25 cm, Jewish Museum, New York.

- Prepare a well-cooked meal of domestic livestock – he'll never know it wasn't venison.

- Wear Esau's gamy-smelling clothing to make blind Isaac think he is speaking to Esau. (Isaac has apparently lost his eyesight, but not his sense of smell.)

- Put goatskin pieces on your arms and neck to simulate Esau's hairiness. (Can you really fool Isaac with fur? Or was Esau that hairy?)

Jacob is afraid that if his father discovers the ruse, he will curse him. "Let the curse fall on me," says his mother. "Just do what I say."

Jacob follows his mother's instructions and thus begins the deception. Isaac seems to suspect something and asks Jacob directly: "Are you really my son Esau?"

"I am," Jacob says without hesitation.

Later, when Isaac realizes what has happened, he calls this deceit. Note the Hebrew play on words in verse 36.

> "³⁵ But he said, 'Your brother came **deceitfully** and took your blessing.' ³⁶ Esau said, 'Isn't he rightly named Jacob (*ya'aqōb*)? He has **deceived** ('*āqab*) me these two times: He took my birthright, and now he's taken my blessing!'" (27:35-36)

"Deceitfully" (NIV, NRSV), "subtilty" (KJV) in verse 35 is *mirmâ*, "deceit, treachery," from the verb *rāmâ*, "beguile, deceive, mislead."[14] Esau remarks that Jacob (whose name means "supplanter, deceiver") has acted in accordance with his name.

Q3. (Genesis 27:6-29) God had told Rebekah that Jacob is supposed to rule over Esau (Genesis 25:23). To what extent does this excuse her plan to deceive her husband Isaac? How much responsibility does Jacob bear in the deception?
http://www.joyfulheart.com/forums/index.php?showtopic=925

Isaac Blesses Jacob (27:27-29)

And so Isaac blesses Jacob with a blessing Isaac had intended for the minutes-older twin Esau. It includes:

- Heaven's dew and earth's richness – an abundance of grain and new wine
- The subjection of whole nations.
- Priority and superiority over his brothers,
- Protection from the curses of others, and
- To be a source of blessing to others.

The key words that Rebekah had sought for were spoken:

"Be lord over your brothers,
and may the sons of your mother bow down to you." (27:29b)

Now Jacob has obtained both the birthright and the coveted blessing from his father. Jacob has won; Esau has lost.

---

[14] William White, *rāmâ*, TWOT #2169d.

When Esau returns too late, his father gives him not a blessing, but a kind of anti-blessing, which is the promise that he will overthrow his brother's domination at some point (27:39-40).

What Kind of Blessing Is This?

What kind of blessing is this? It is clear from Isaac's reaction when he discovers the deception ("violent trembling," 27:33), that he didn't realize he was pronouncing the blessing on the wrong person.

It becomes clear that this is more than the simple blessing of a father to a son. It is a kind of spoken prophecy that comes from the Lord himself, given through Isaac as a spokesman to the person God intends to bless. We see two additional examples later in Genesis, which we'll study in detail in Lesson 7.

- Jacob's blessing of Joseph's sons, Ephraim and Manasseh (Genesis 48)
- Jacob's blessing of his twelve sons (Genesis 49)

In each case Jacob prophesies a specific blessing, speaking of future things that he has no way of knowing except for God's word in his mouth.

In one sense, Isaac's blessing of Jacob and Esau is God's, not Isaac's. In that case, I wonder if Rebekah's and Jacob's deceitful intervention was "necessary," if God would have blessed Jacob in spite of Isaac's intentions to the contrary? Some of Isaac's blessing of Jacob might be attributed to a father's good wishes for his firstborn, but there's more. Isaac's later blessing of Esau includes at least one phrase that sounds much like prophecy:

> "You will live by the sword
> and you will serve your brother.
> But when you grow restless,
> you will throw his yoke from off your neck." (27:40)

Indeed, Esau later does prevent Jacob from ruling over him. But Esau does not attempt to subjugate Jacob, even when he had a chance. We'll explore that further in Lesson 4.

> Q4. (Genesis 27:33) Why couldn't Isaac reverse his blessing once he discovers Jacob's trickery? What is Isaac's role in this blessing? What is God's role in it?
> http:/www.joyfulheart.com/forums/index.php?showtopic=926

Can God bless through Unrighteousness

Of course, there's an ethical problem with Rebekah's and Jacob's deception. If God is a God of truth, then this is the opposite of truth. It is a sin. It is unrighteous. And though it is quite in keeping with Jacob's opportunistic and deceptive character so far, it is hardly worthy of approval – except perhaps by shrewd people who value expediency over integrity.

Can God – does God – allow sin to be a part of the working out of his purposes? The surprising answer of Genesis is, "Yes." Later in Genesis we come to the sordid tale of Joseph's brothers selling him into slavery out of jealously. After Jacob's death his brother's are terrified. Listen to Joseph's answer:

> "You intended to harm me, but God intended it for good to accomplish what is now being done, the saving of many lives." (50:20)

Though Joseph's brothers had sold him into slavery with the basest of motives, and a clear sin against him and against their father, "God intended it for good...." Does this mean that somehow Joseph's brothers are innocent, that God made them do it and they had no choice? No. They were responsible for their sin, just as Judas was responsible for his sin, even though in his sin he was fulfilling prophecy.

God's sovereignty and man's free will

We see human sin and responsibility on the one side and God working out his plan on the other. Of course, we're getting deep into things we scarcely understand. We throw around such words as predestination, foreknowledge, foreordination, and the like, as if we understood them. They are merely theological constructs to label what we've never experienced firsthand. Whole churches have been divided over views of God's sovereignty and man's will. There's no need to re-visit these sorry controversies.

But to be biblical and balanced we must affirm two seemingly contrary truths:

1. God is sovereign
2. Man has a free will

Both are somehow true.

> "And we know that in all things God works for the good of those who love him, who have been called according to his purpose." (Romans 8:28)

In spite of man's evil, God will still work good out of it and further his plan in spite of it. True, man's evil causes great pain and suffering, which God does not always shield us from – nor did he shield his own Son – but he will work out his plan.

I struggle against saying about every tragedy, "It must be God's will." Many times tragedies are the result of man's sin. But I can affirm that God can work good out of every tragedy. Indeed, he delights in doing so!

Preferring One Child over Another (25:28)

Rebekah loved Jacob, while Isaac loved Esau (25:28). What trouble this caused! Jacob himself made the same mistake by loving the sons of his beloved wife Rachel – Joseph and Benjamin – to the obvious pain and jealously of their brothers. Later, David makes a similar mistake to the ruin of *his* family.

As parents, we need to learn from this. While we cannot love our children the same, we must love them equally if we desire a peaceful household and children whose lives are blessed. Of course, each child is different and we show our love in different ways to them. Love is the key.

> Q5. (Genesis 25:28) What happens when your children sense that you love one child more than another? Did such discrimination happen to you when you were growing up? If so, how are you finding healing? How can we as parents love our children equally but differently?
> http:/www.joyfulheart.com/forums/index.php?showtopic=927

"Jacob Have I loved"

We can't leave this passage without looking for a moment at God's preference of Jacob over Esau. Esau was a descendent of Abraham, but didn't have the spiritual acuity to appreciate it. Though God blessed Esau's descendents with nation-status, the country of Edom, they were subjugated again and again by the sons of Jacob (Israel).

Here we really get into the thick of predestination. In explaining God's sovereignty in Romans 9:10-13, Paul uses Jacob and Esau as examples, quoting Malachi:

> "'Was not Esau Jacob's brother?' the LORD says.
> 'Yet I have **loved** Jacob,
> but Esau I have **hated**,
> and I have turned his mountains into a wasteland
> and left his inheritance to the desert jackals.'" (Malachi 1:2-3)

This indicates, says the Apostle Paul, "... that God's purpose in election might stand: not by works, but by him who calls" (Romans 9:11b-12a). "It does not, therefore, depend on man's desire or effort," Paul concludes, "but on God's mercy" (Roman 9:16).

God is in ultimate control and we can't do anything about it. This is hard for us humans. We don't like anyone taking away our control over our destiny – not even God!

Did God really *love* Jacob and *hate* Esau? No. God loved them both, but for his plan of redemption, he *preferred* Jacob over Esau, and decided to bring the blessings of Abraham to the entire world through the offspring of Jacob rather than Esau. "Love" and "hate" are used hyperbolically in place of "prefer" or "show favor" in order to make a point.

It's pretty obvious that neither Jacob nor Esau had a sterling character. God didn't chose Jacob over Esau because Jacob was more righteous. God had a plan in spite of Jacob's character. God works on Jacob's character and changes it, as we'll see, but God's plan and purpose for Jacob is not dependent upon Jacob's goodness and worthiness, but on God's grace and plan.

Q6. Extra Credit. Whose character flaws most remind you of your own? Isaac's, Rebekah's, Esau's, or Jacob's? Why? How is God working to improve your character?
http://www.joyfulheart.com/forums/index.php?showtopic=928

Conclusion

While we haven't got all our questions answered, this passage gives us lots to think about, to grasp insights about character and personal growth. What have we learned?

- There is hope for flawed people such as us.
- God's choice to bless us is based on his own purposes, not on ours.

This should give us hope. God has made clear in the New Testament that he intends to bless us in spite of ourselves, in spite of our flawed character. He is faithful to us, not for our sakes alone, but for the sake of Jesus who died for us to redeem us.

Prayer

Father, as the story of Jacob and Esau unfolds, I find that both of them have deep flaws. When I'm honest, I see deep flaws in myself. I ask you to heal what is broken in me. And work in me and through me, not based on my righteousness, but by the mercies of Jesus. In His name, I pray. Amen.

2. Jacob Meets God (Genesis 27:41-28:22)

Every action we take, for good or for bad, has a reaction. The reaction to Jacob's deceit is enmity with his brother Esau. It doesn't matter that Jacob's sin led to a fulfillment of the will of God, there is still a reaction.

Esau's Grudge (27:41)

> "Esau held a grudge against Jacob because of the blessing his father had given him. He said to himself, 'The days of mourning for my father are near; then I will kill my brother Jacob.'" (27:41)

Fortunately for Jacob, Isaac lives another 44 years or so. But Esau's sin of murder in his heart is yet another occasion to move Jacob into the center of God's will for him, to find him wives in Haran who will bear the 12 sons, whose descendants will constitute the 12 tribes of Israel. Strange, how God can work out his will through sin, in spite of sin! This is a mystery to us.

Yet, here it is. Esau bears a grudge and because of this grudge begins to speak about his intentions to others. Note: first he says it to himself (27:41), but soon he is saying it to others (27:42). Out of the abundance of the heart, the mouth speaks.

James J. Tissot, "Jacob's Dream" (c. 1896-1902), gouache on board, Jewish Museum, New York.

Rebekah's Plan (27:42-45)

> "⁴² When Rebekah was told what her older son Esau had said, she sent for her younger son Jacob and said to him, 'Your brother Esau is consoling himself with the thought of killing you. ⁴³ Now then, my son, do what I say: Flee at once to my brother Laban in Haran. ⁴⁴ Stay with him for a while until your brother's fury subsides. ⁴⁵ When your brother is no longer angry with you and forgets what you did to him, I'll send word for you to come back from there. Why should I lose both of you in one day?'" (27:42-45)

2. Jacob Meets God (Genesis 27:41-28:22)

Rebekah overhears what Esau is plotting against her favorite son, and summons Jacob. "Flee at once," is her command. Is running from our enemies ever an answer? Sometimes. On a number of occasions when Jesus' enemies sought to arrest him or stone him, he just slipped away in the crowd (Luke 4:30; John 8:59; 10:39). Jesus had a mission to complete, and showdowns with his enemies did not suit this mission. Too often, our ego is so involved that we refuse to avoid conflicts which would distract us from our primary task. Jacob's primary task – from God's perspective – is to become a man of God and to raise a big family. He can do that better in Haran than he could with the Canaanite women in Palestine at the time. So Esau's threat becomes the impetus for change.

Godly Marriage

Esau had married two wives from among the local heathen tribes populating Palestine at that time, the Hittites.

> "When Esau was forty years old, he married Judith daughter of Beeri the Hittite, and also Basemath daughter of Elon the Hittite. They were a source of grief to Isaac and Rebekah." (26:34-35).

We aren't told the source of the conflict, but it is, no doubt, partly cultural. Rebekah has been raised in a nomadic tribe hundreds of miles away in Haran (Paddan Aram), north of the Euphrates River. The Hittites lived in houses and cities, and had different values. Probably Esau had brought his wives to live in the family encampment near Beersheba (26:23, 33). "We hate living in tents," they may have complained. "Things used to be better in our home cities." Complain, complain, complain. Major in-law conflicts result from this cross-cultural marriage.

Religion of the Canaanites

Not that Rebekah's family have been faithful followers of Yahweh, the God of Abraham. They possess household idols and are probably moon worshippers (31:19; Joshua 24:2, 15; see the Introduction). Apparently God preferred converting people from this distortion of true worship, than from the distortions practiced by the Canaanites. If the Israelites' religion were too close to that of the tribes of Canaan, the Israelites would be more tempted than ever to assimilate heathen practices into their worship.

Polygamy in the Ancient Near East

Esau has two wives. Eventually, Jacob acquires two wives and two concubines. Today Muslims allow up to four wives, if the husband is wealthy enough to support them. In the ancient Near East, having a number of wives was considered a mark of wealth and power. David had six wives, plus a number of concubines. Solomon had more than 1,000 wives and concubines (and he was considered wise!). But these multiple-wife households were full of problems of jealousy and favoritism, as we will see as our story unfolds. The Bible doesn't seek to justify polygamy, only report it.

What are we as Christians to think about polygamy? "In the beginning it was not so," said Jesus (Matthew 19:8b). He taught:

> "At the beginning the Creator 'made them male and female,' and said, 'For this reason a man will leave his father and mother and be united to his wife, and the two will become one flesh.' So they are no longer two, but one." (Matthew 19:4-6, quoting Genesis 2:24)

Monogamy is God's ideal, the righteous standard. But perhaps due to the hardness of men's hearts (Matthew 19:8), God allowed polygamy for a time. Certainly by the mid-first century AD, the Christian standard was "the husband of but one wife" (1 Timothy 3:2; Titus 1:6). This is still an issue in Africa, where, in many cultures, polygamy has been practiced for many generations. Typically, by the second generation of Christians in a believing family, polygamy is no longer practiced.

Jacob Is Sent Away to Find a Wife (27:46-28:2)

Rebekah is the master manipulator. She knows how to get her way – with Isaac, with Esau, and with Jacob. She says to Isaac:

> "I'm disgusted with living because of these Hittite women. If Jacob takes a wife from among the women of this land, from Hittite women like these, my life will not be worth living." (27:46)

Isaac, too, has suffered from having Esau's wives around (26:35). He takes action:

> "So Isaac called for Jacob and blessed him and commanded him: 'Do not marry a Canaanite woman. Go at once to Paddan Aram, to the house of your mother's father Bethuel. Take a wife for yourself there, from among the daughters of Laban, your mother's brother." (28:1-2)

Now, Jacob can flee Esau with an excuse and with his father's blessing. Esau, too, hears of his father's wishes regarding a non-Hittite wife for Jacob, so Esau finds a descendent of Abraham – Mahalath, Ishmael's daughter – and marries her as a third wife, in order to try to please his father (28:6-9).

The Blessing of Abraham (28:3-4)

In spite of Jacob openly deceiving his father, Isaac still loves him and blesses him generously as he departs. Perhaps Isaac is finally beginning to see that Jacob is indeed the son through whom God's promise to Abraham will be fulfilled. And so he speaks over Jacob the ancient blessing of Abraham:

> "³ May God Almighty bless you and make you fruitful and increase your numbers until you become a community of peoples. ⁴ May he give you and your descendants the blessing given to Abraham, so that you may take possession of the land where you now live as an alien, the land God gave to Abraham." (28:3-4)

Look carefully at the blessing, for it is a central theme of both the Old Testament and the New. This is the same blessing that God gave Abraham more than a century before Jacob's departure for Haran. In the chart below you can see the various forms of this blessing. There are at least three elements woven again and again through these blessings:

1. Fruitfulness – numerous descendants,
2. Land – the land of Canaan, and
3. World – the nations of the world will be blessed.

	Descendants	Land	Blessing of nations
God to Abraham in Haran (12:2-3)	x		x
God to Abraham at Hebron (15:1-21)	x	x	
God to Abraham at Hebron (17:1-21)	x	x	
God to Abraham at Hebron (18:17)	x		x
God to Abraham at Mt. Moriah (22:15-18)	x		x
God to Isaac at Gerar (26:2-5)	x	x	x
God to Isaac at Beersheba (26:24)	x		x
Isaac to Jacob at Beersheba (27:27-29)			x
Isaac to Jacob at Beersheba (28:3-4)	x	x	

	Descendants	Land	Blessing of nations
God to Jacob at Bethel (28:13-15)	x	x	x
God to Jacob at Bethel (35:11-12)	x	x	

This series of blessings introduces concepts that anchor themselves in Genesis and carry on throughout the Bible: covenant – blessings and cursings, oaths and promises. We'll examine these more fully in Lesson 7.

The blessing of Abraham is mentioned in the New Testament also:

> "[Christ] redeemed us in order that the blessing given to Abraham might come to the Gentiles through Christ Jesus, so that by faith we might receive the promise of the Spirit." (Galatians 3:14)

> "If you belong to Christ, then you are Abraham's seed, and heirs according to the promise." (Galatians 3:29)

Paul's argument is that Jesus is the Seed of Abraham, and if we belong to Jesus, then we, too, are descendants and heirs of Abraham. So what of Abraham's promise is left for us to inherit?

1. **Land**. Christ will reign on earth from Jerusalem, we are told.

2. **Descendants**. For us, probably spiritual descendents are most prominent.

3. **World**. Abraham's spiritual descendents are the salt of the earth who bring the message of Abraham's Seed – the Messiah – to the world. We are to be a blessing to the world. Through us, Christ's blessings are to flow out to others.

Q1. (Genesis 28:3-4) Why does Isaac bless Jacob, especially after Jacob's deception? How does this blessing compare to other blessings of Abraham, Isaac, and Jacob? What are the main elements of Isaac's blessing?
http://www.joyfulheart.com/forums/index.php?showtopic=929

2. Jacob Meets God (Genesis 27:41-28:22)

Jacob Begins His Journey (28:10-11)

> "Then Isaac sent Jacob on his way, and he went to Paddan Aram, to Laban son of Bethuel the Aramean, the brother of Rebekah, who was the mother of Jacob and Esau." (28:5)

> "Jacob left Beersheba and set out for Haran. When he reached a certain place, he stopped for the night because the sun had set.... He called that place Bethel, though the city used to be called Luz." (28:10-11, 19)

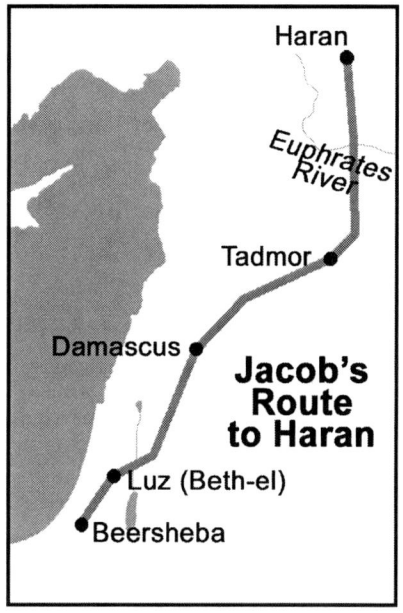

Jacob leaves Isaac's tent in Beersheba, a desert town in the extreme south of Palestine, and heads north to his uncle's home, hundreds of miles away around the Fertile Crescent. He stops, perhaps the second or third night, at a town called Luz (28:19).

Jacob's Dream (28:11-12)

> "¹¹ When he reached a certain place, he stopped for the night because the sun had set. Taking one of the stones there, he put it under his head and lay down to sleep. ¹² He had a dream in which he saw a stairway resting on the earth, with its top reaching to heaven, and the angels of God were ascending and descending on it." (28:11-12)

As he sleeps, he sees a vision of "Jacob's Ladder," angels ascending and descending a ladder or stairway[1] to heaven itself, with the base of it resting near him – the "gateway" of heaven.

God's Blessing in the Dream (28:13-15)

Then, in the dream, God himself appears to Jacob and speaks.

---

[1] *Sullām*, "ladder." Patterson remarks, "Some would suggest the translation "stairway" and liken the structure to a ziggurat, which is possible. However, there are other words for stairway, and ladders were used at a very early time" (R.D. Patterson, *Sullām*, TWOT #1506c). However, Hamilton sees a connection (through metathesis) with the Akkadian *simmiltu*, "stairway" (Hamilton, *Genesis*, p. 239).

> "¹³ᵇ I am the LORD, the God of your father Abraham and the God of Isaac.
> I will give you and your descendants the land on which you are lying.
> ¹⁴ Your descendants will be like the dust of the earth,
> and you will spread out to the west and to the east, to the north and to the south.
> All peoples on earth will be blessed through you and your offspring.
> ¹⁵ I am with you and will watch over you wherever you go, and I will bring you back to this land. I will not leave you until I have done what I have promised you."
> (28:13-15)

First, **God identifies himself**: "I am the LORD, the God of your father Abraham and the God of Isaac" (28:13b).

Second, he renews the promise of **inheritance of the land** of Canaan:

> "I will give you and your descendants the land on which you are lying." (28:13c)

Third, he promises a multitude of **descendants**:

> "Your descendants will be like the dust of the earth, and you will spread out² to the west and to the east, to the north and to the south." (28:14a)

Fourth, he promises that Jacob and his offspring will be a **source of blessing** to the entire world:

> "All peoples on earth will be blessed through you and your offspring." (28:14b)

William Blake (1757-1827), "Jacob's Ladder" (1800), watercolor, 37 x 29 cm, British Museum.

As we've seen, these promises form the core of the promises made to Abraham, renewed to Isaac, and then passed on to Jacob.

But he goes on to make **personal promises to Jacob**:

> "I am with you and will watch over³ you wherever you go, and I will bring you back to this land. I will not leave you until I have done what I have promised you." (28:15)

This doesn't mean that God will eventually leave him; it means that God will be with him to fulfill the promise.

---

² *Pāraṣ*, "break through," perhaps here, "spread," that is, "become known." (BDB 829, 10).
³ *Shāmar*, "keep, preserve, protect" (BDB 1036, 4).

Hundreds of years later, after the tabernacle had been built and the people settled in Canaan, such pillars were not allowed (Deuteronomy 16:21). They were too easily confused with the heathen Baal worship which occurred on the high places, in contrast to the true worship of Yahweh.

But in Jacob's time, the setting up of such a commemorative stele or pillar seemed an entirely appropriate way to honor and remember God's revelation of himself in this place.[8] Prior to this time, his father Isaac had led the family in worship of Yahweh. But for the first time Jacob sets upright a stone of faith and remembrance before the Lord. It is his way of placing himself, his life, before the Lord. His father's God has become his own God now.

Anointing the Stone (28:18b)

After Jacob sets up the stone, he pours on top of it some of the precious oil he had taken with him for his journey.

Jacob sets up a stone to the Lord, unknown illustrator.

The practice of anointing seemed to be involved with cleansing and consecrating to God. Centuries later, kings, priests, and prophets were anointed for their offices. Objects in the tabernacle were anointed with specially-formulated anointing oil: altars, the tent of meeting, the ark, the laver and its stand, and all objects relating to the altar.[9] When Samuel anoints David as king over Israel, the scripture records, "from that day on the Spirit of the LORD came upon David in power" (1 Samuel 16:13). The words "Messiah" (Hebrew *māshîah*) and Christ (Greek *christos*) both mean "Anointed One." Peter describes "how God anointed Jesus of Nazareth with the Holy Spirit and power...." (Acts 10:38).

---

[8] Roland K. Harrison, "pillar," *ISBE* 3:869-871; Roland de Vaux, *Ancient Israel* 2:285-286; Uzi Avner, "Scared Stones in the Desert," *Biblical Archaeology Review*, May-June 2001..Such a stone is known by different names: pillar, standing stone, massebah, and stele. See also passages in Genesis 31:13, 45, 51f; 35:14,20; Exodus 23:24; 24:4; 34:13; Deuteronomy 7:5; 12:3; 16:22, etc.

[9] Franz Hesse, *chrio TDNT* 9:496-509.

So Jacob sets up the stone as an act of dedication of himself in worship, a way of remembering God's presence in this place. He anoints it as an act of cleansing and consecration, setting it – and himself – apart for God.

Jacob's Holy Vow to Yahweh (28:20-22)

But Jacob's act of commitment to Yahweh is not over yet. It includes a vow.

"[20] Then Jacob made a vow, saying, 'If God will be with me and will watch over me on this journey I am taking and will give me food to eat and clothes to wear [21] so that I return safely to my father's house, then the LORD will be my God [22] and this stone that I have set up as a pillar will be God's house, and of all that you give me I will give you a tenth.'" (28:20-22)

Here are the provisions of the vow. Notice the giant "if" clauses:

- If God will be with me...
- If God will watch over (protect) me...
- If God will give me food and clothing...
- If God brings me safely again to my father's house ...

If God will do what he has promised, then Jacob solemnly vows:

- Then Yahweh will be my God...
- Then this pillar will be God's house...
- Then I will give God a tenth of all God gives me.

This may look like bargaining with God, but such was the format of a formal vow in Jacob's time. Each party would state his obligations and rights and formally make a vow to uphold the covenant. God has made promises to him in the dream; now Jacob formally responds. Yahweh has been his father's God, but now he vows that Yahweh (and Yahweh alone) will be his own God. What was family tradition now becomes personal.

"Vow" is *nēder*, "the act of verbally consecrating to (devoting to the service of) God, that is, vowing to perform.... To bind one's self with what proceeds from one's mouth."[10]

---

[10] "A *nēder* is something promised to God verbally" (Leonard J. Coppes, *nādar*, TWOT #1308a).

The Promise to Return to Canaan (28:15b, 21a)

Notice one consistent element of both God's promise and Jacob's vow: return.[11]

"I will **bring you back** to this land." (28:15b)

"... so that I **return** safely to my father's house...." (28:21a)

God's purpose for Jacob is focused in Canaan, the land that God had promised to Abraham and his descendents forever. However, the present journey is not just a sidebar to Jacob's life. Sometimes we feel like God may put us on a shelf, or that we're off on a siding, rather than on the main track. We must be patient as God works out his purposes in our lives. We can't always see God's purposes from our vantage point. We must trust him. He will "bring us back" safely to that place he has for us.

Q3. (Genesis 28:18-21) What did it mean to Jacob to set up the stone? What did anointing the stone mean to him? Why does he do these things? What does he promise God in his vow?
http://www.joyfulheart.com/forums/index.php?showtopic=931

Jacob Promises to Tithe (28:22)

"... Of all that you give me I will give you a tenth." (28:22)

Why does Jacob promise to tithe, that is, give one tenth of all that God gives him? His grandfather Abraham had tithed to Melchizedek, king of (Jeru)salem and priest of the Most High God (14:18-20), so there is some family tradition. But what does tithing mean in this context?

---

[11] The very common verb *shûb* is used in both verses. The basic meaning of *shûb* in the Qal stem (as in verse 21a) is "to (re)turn," implying physical motion or movement. The Hiphil stem (as in verse 15b) is causative, "bring back, carry back" (Victor P. Hamilton, *shûb*, TWOT #2340).

Tithing was known outside of Israel in the Near East. For example, we hear of tithing among the Egyptians, Syrians, Lydians, Babylonians, Assyrians, and in Ugarit and Carthage. But these tithes were not all religious; some were taxation by the king.[12]

Tithing as Allegiance to a King

We see an interesting passage in 1 Samuel 8, where the Israelites demand that the aging prophet Samuel give them "a king to lead us, such as all the other nations have" (1 Samuel 8:5). The Lord tells Samuel, "It is not you they have rejected, but they have rejected me as their king" (1 Samuel 8:7). So Samuel warns them about what a king will require of them:

> "... He will take a tenth of your grain and of your vintage and give it to his officials and attendants...." (1 Samuel 8:15)

I believe that Jacob offering to tithe is his way of accepting the Lord's kingship over him, an act of submission and fealty.

This would accord well with Israel's tithe after the tabernacle was built, as well. If you study it, you'll see that the tabernacle in the wilderness was built as a richly appointed portable palace for Israel's invisible king. The Holy of Holies was the throne room, where the Mercy Seat was over the Ark of the Covenant, the throne. The next room was the Holy Place where the Levitical Priests attended the King, burning incense on the golden Altar of Incense, keeping the Seven-Branched Lampstand lit, and bringing fresh loaves for the Table of Showbread. The courtyard which surrounded the Tabernacle formed a boundary of sacred ground in the very midst of Israel's camp.

Tithes were collected from the people in order to support the Levites who served the God in the tabernacle or temple.

> "I give to the Levites all the tithes in Israel as their inheritance in return for the work they do while serving at the Tent of Meeting." (Numbers 18:21)

Through the Prophet Malachi, God says that to withhold the tithe is to rob God (Malachi 3:8). The tithe was not just an offering to God, but his due.

> "Bring the whole tithe into the storehouse, that there may be food in my house." (Malachi 3:10a)

---

[12] Eugene E. Carpenter, "Tithe," ISBE 4:861-864.

2. Jacob Meets God (Genesis 27:41-28:22)

Tithing as a Recognition of God's Supply

So Jacob says:

"... Of all that **you give** me I will give you a tenth." (28:22)

Jacob's faith is both that God will supply – and that the resources are ultimately God's. His tithe is a recognition of that.

My point is that Jacob's vow to tithe all that God gives him is both a statement of faith that God will meet his needs, and a vow of loyalty and submission to the Lord as his King and God. (When you ask *who* Jacob ended up tithing to, however, I run out of answers.)

I believe that tithing for the Christian represents something similar. We see ourselves as stewards of what actually belongs to God. And the tithe of our income is a way of demonstrating our allegiance, our love, and that we serve God rather than Money (Matthew 6:24).

Ultimately, tithing isn't about money but about discipleship. Tithing is a powerful indicator to us that we trust God and have committed our lives to him. And so it was for Jacob.

Q4. (Genesis 28:22) What does Jacob's promise to tithe indicate about his commitment? Presumably, Jacob has been a believer in Yahweh all his life. In what sense is this incident at Bethel a conversion experience for him? What is the relationship of tithing to conversion?
http://www.joyfulheart.com/forums/index.php?showtopic=932

At the beginning of our passage we see Jacob the manipulator fleeing from his brother. But before he gets very far, he meets God and his life is radically changed. He has heard about his father's God; now he meets him. He had heard of the blessings of Abraham; now he has them renewed to him by God himself. He has had a nebulous faith in his father's God; now he commits himself in allegiance and submission to God as his King and Lord. Jacob the Supplanter is converted.

Prayer

Lord God, thank you for your patient love that finds us and calls us to yourself. I pray that my conversion to serve you might be deep and lasting. I place myself before you as Jacob set up a stone in your sight. I offer my tithe to you as a way of saying that I place myself under you and give you my full allegiance and trust. I love you. In Jesus' name, I pray. Amen.

3. Jacob and Laban, Rachel and Leah (Genesis 29-31)

God hasn't forgotten Jacob's flaws. He has very definite plans to mould Jacob's heart. Someone once said, "God catches his fish before he cleans them." God has "caught" Jacob. Now we'll watch as he cleans him.

The Supplanter, whose cheating forced him to leave his home, now arrives in Paddan Aram (Haran), hundreds of miles away. He is lonely, and eager to see his mother's family, hoping that they will receive him into their home.

Lesson 3 covers three chapters. It's a wonderfully written story, so be sure to read it in your Bible. We'll be looking at the highlights.

Haran

Haran lies along the Jullab River just inside present day Turkey near its border with Iraq, 24 miles southeast of the Turkish city Urfa, and 60 miles north of the Euphrates River. It is located on the main road that ran from Nineveh to Carchemish and was considered a strategic city in ancient times. Its chief cult was that of the Mesopotamian moon-god Sin. It was probably founded as a merchant outpost by the Sumerian city of Ur in the late third millennium BC. The name Haran means "highway, road, caravan" in Akkadian.

James J. Tissot, " Jacob and Rachel at the Well" (c. 1896-1902), gouache on board, 26.4 x 21 cm, Jewish Museum, New York.

Today a village on this site consists of beehive shaped houses. There is only a small amount of archaeological evidence available, but it includes inscriptional evidence of the Sin temple (from the beginning of the second millennium), a stella of the moon-god, and violent destruction about 610 BC by the Scythians, Medes, and Chaldeans.[1]

---

[1] Mark W. Chavalas, "Haran," DOTP 379-381; Robert J. Hughes, III, "Haran," ISBE 2:614.

Jacob's Family in Haran

I've included a family tree of Abraham's ancestors and descendents so you can see Jacob's place in it and get an idea of the various family relationships between Rachel's family and Isaac's.

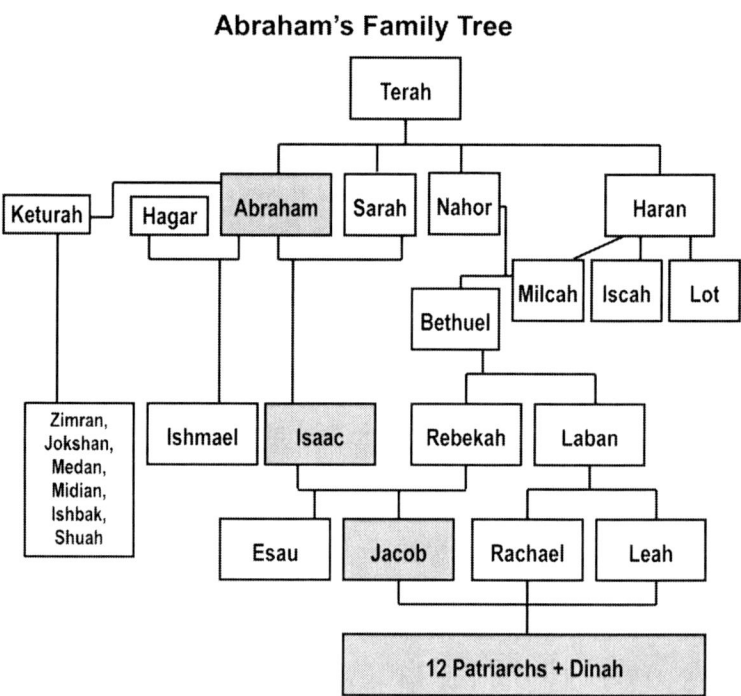

Jacob the Servant (29:1-14)

Jacob arrives at a well in the desert to find three flocks of sheep lying near it and their shepherds taking their ease.

"Have you heard of Laban?" he asks.

"Yes, we know him."

"How is he?"

"He's fine ... and here comes his daughter Rachel."

Jacob sees a young woman leading a flock of sheep towards the well, looks at the heavy stone over the well, and suddenly he feels a chivalrous impulse towards his cousin.

"Get up," he says to the reclining shepherds, hoping to get them to move the stone. "It's not quitting time. Water the sheep and then take them back in the field. There's still time for grazing before dark."

None makes a move. "We always wait until all the flocks are gathered before we move the stone and water the sheep," they tell him. They don't move a muscle. They wait for all the shepherds to arrive before they move the stone together. No need to hurry today.

3. Jacob and Laban, Rachel and Leah (Genesis 29-31)

So Jacob goes to the well alone. The God who has promised to be with him gives him power. Single-handedly, by a great feat of strength, he rolls the great stone away from the top of the well. Then he puts down the bucket again and again to fill the nearby trough, until all of Rachel's sheep have been watered. Only when he's finished does the mysterious stranger identify himself. He kisses her in the Eastern custom of greeting and begins to weep.

"I am Jacob," he says, overcome by emotion. "Your father's nephew and Rebekah's son."

She runs home to tell her father of the wonderful man who has helped her water her sheep, a long lost relative. Soon Laban hurries to the well, embraces Jacob, kisses him, and invites him home, inquiring about the welfare of his sister and the rest of the Western branch of the family. "You are my own flesh and blood," he says.

Love Is Blind (29:15-30)

And so Jacob enjoys the comfort of his mother's family and helps out with the chores. But by his moving of the well stone, Jacob has shown them that he is a doer, a decisive person, a strong man. He could be useful, thinks Laban. A month goes by, and one evening Laban brings up the matter of staying.

William Dyce (English pre-Raphaelite painter, 1806-1864), "The Meeting of Jacob and Rachel" (before 1850), oil on canvas, 36 x 46 cm, private collection.

Laban isn't blind. He has observed how Jacob looks at his daughter and she at him. He sees a man utterly entranced. So he brings up the matter of wages.

"Just because you are kin doesn't mean I shouldn't be paying you for your work," he begins. "Let's determine some basis to pay you wages for watching my flocks."

Jacob has no doubt been thinking about this very thing. He has no money for a bride price, but he must have this enchanting girl, "lovely in form, and beautiful" (29:17).

"I'll work seven years for you in return for your younger daughter Rachel," he ventures.

Laban couldn't have hoped for more. Seven years of labor just for a bride price? That was far too generous. He must love her! But Laban doesn't let on.

"It'd be better for me to give her to *you* than some other man," he says with feigned resignation. "Stay with me." And so Jacob stays and works seven years for the love of his life, "but they seemed like only a few days to him because of his love for her" (29:20).

At the end of seven years – and I'm sure Jacob has been counting – he says to Laban, "Give me my wife. My time is completed, and I want to lie with her" (29:21). That's a pretty direct way to talk to the father-of-the-bride!

Laban calls all his friends for a sumptuous feast to celebrate the event. The party goes long into the night. But Laban sends Leah, not Rachel, to Jacob's tent to enjoy a night of intimacy. The scripture is terse: "When morning came, there was Leah!" (29:25). What a shock!

How could it have happened? Apparently customs of the time required no formal wedding ceremony to precede the consummation. Laban had called a feast (Hebrew *mishteh*, from the root *shātâ*, "to drink"), a drinking banquet.[2] Jacob was "both in drink and in the dark," concluded Jewish historian Josephus.[3] This isn't the first time in Scripture that this sort of thing occurred; Lot's daughters had become pregnant by their father after getting him drunk (19:32-35).

You can't miss the irony. Jacob deceives his blind father into believing he is Esau and giving him the blessing, and so Laban deceives the deceiver into marrying the older sister instead the girl of his dreams.

Jacob comes to Laban in the morning in anger. "What is this you have done to me? I served you for Rachel, didn't I? Why have you tricked me?"

Laban replies evenly, "Didn't you know? Here in Haran it is our custom to marry off the older daughter before the younger." You can almost see him smile wickedly, his yellowing teeth showing as he grins. "But I have such a deal for you. Spend the customary bridal week with Leah, and at the end of the week you can have Rachel. Only seven years more labor for her. What's a little misunderstanding among kin?"

Jacob is burning inwardly, but he sees his prize in sight. Only a week. He agrees to Laban's offer, and soon Rachel is his. Jacob's story gives new meaning to the saying "Love is blind."

---

[2] Hermann J. Austel, *shātâ*, TWOT #2477c.
[3] Josephus, *Antiquities of the Jews*, 1.19.7.

3. Jacob and Laban, Rachel and Leah (Genesis 29-31)

Jacob's Children (29:31-30:24)

Why, I wonder, does God allow Jacob to be tricked? I'm sure that the Supplanter needs to taste some of his own medicine. God is building a character of integrity in Jacob and God needs to deal with this serious flaw of deceit.

But this is more than character building. This is also a time of family building. God is raising up for Jacob the beginnings of the great people that he had promised, as many as the sand of the seashore and the stars in the sky. God begins the Israelite people with the gene pool of five individuals, three of them closely related (Jacob, Leah, and Rachel), and two of them completely different, the servant girls (Bilhah and Zilpah).

James J. Tissot, "Rachel and Leah" (c. 1896-1902), gouache on board, Jewish Museum, New York.

Q1. (Genesis 29) Why do you think God allows Jacob to be tricked into 14 years of labor for two wives? What purposes do you think God is working out through these circumstances?
http://www.joyfulheart.com/forums/index.php?showtopic=933

As a wedding present Laban gives each of his daughters a maidservant as their property. Leah is given Zilpah (29:24), and Rachel is given Bilhah (29:29). The Scripture doesn't teach slavery any more than polygamy, but God works within people and cultures in spite of their institutional sins and gradually changes them and their values. The Scripture simply reports here.

The passage that recounts each of Jacob's children unfolds a tale of jealousy and competition within the family, though we'll be skipping over most of the details.

Rachel is the favorite wife, but is barren (29:30). She gives up Jacob to her sister's bed in exchange for mandrakes, reputed to make a woman fertile, but to no avail (30:14-16). She is reduced to giving her servant Bilhah to Jacob to bear children for her (30:1-6), and when Leah's fecundity falters, Leah reciprocates by giving her servant girl Zilpah to Jacob to bear still more children (30:9).

Bilhah and Zilpah don't have full status as wives, since they are clearly acting as surrogates for their mistresses. Notice, for example, who names the babies. They would be considered concubines. However, the children all seem to have equal status as Jacob's offspring.

We see in this passage an interesting custom of naming of children based on the hopes and dreams and happenstances of the wives. In many cases, the derivation of the name is based more on what it "sounds like" than on true etymological derivation, but in a non-literate culture, who knew or cared? Here are the sons, their name meanings, and mothers, given in order of birth.

	Name	Meaning	Mother
1.	Reuben	"see, a son"	Leah
2.	Simeon	"one who hears"	Leah
3.	Levi	"attached"	Leah
4.	Judah	"praise"	Leah
5.	Dan	"he has vindicated"	Bilhah
6.	Naphtali	"my struggle"	Bilhah
7.	Gad	"good fortune" or "a troop"	Zilpah
8.	Asher	"happy"	Zilpah
9.	Issachar	"reward"	Leah
10.	Zebulun	"honor"	Leah
11.	Joseph	"may he add"	Rachel
12.	Benjamin	"son of my right hand" (35:18)	Rachel

I include Benjamin in this list for the sake of completeness, though he is born much later (35:16).

Leah also had a daughter named Dinah, whose name seems to mean "justice" (30:21). Weren't there any other daughters among all these children? Probably. "Daughters" (plural) are mentioned (34:9, 16; 37:35), but they probably weren't considered important to this story of the origins of the Twelve Tribes of Israel. Dinah is mentioned because she figures in family events in chapter 34. Neither were many daughters counted among the members of Jacob's family that went to Egypt (46:8-27). Women figure much more prominently in the New Testament, as Jesus elevates them to equality and importance.

It is clear that Jacob loves only Rachel, but by the time chapter 30 concludes, Jacob is the father of eleven sons and at least one daughter. God has blessed the man!

Jacob Negotiates with Laban (30:25-36)

The birth of these children apparently took a total of fourteen years or more (30:25-26). With a dozen children, two wives, and two concubines to support, Jacob has nothing but his own labor. His family is living off his father-in-law's household income. He is a son-in-law and, as such, has no prospect of inheriting after Laban dies. The property will go to Laban's sons. Jacob owns no flocks. He confronts Laban, asking to be released to return to his homeland, saying, "When may I do something for my own household?" (30:30).

Laban, who likes this sweet deal he has had for years, doesn't want to let him go.

> "'Please stay, for I have learned by divination that the LORD has blessed me because of you.' And he added, 'Name your wages and I will pay them.'" (30:27-28)

The word "divination" (NIV, NRSV), "experience" (KJV) is *nāḥash*, "seek and give an omen, practice divination."[4] Divination is the heathen act of gaining understanding about the present or future by means of signs or omens.[5]

Indeed, Laban had been blessed through Jacob's presence in answer to God's promise, "All peoples on earth will be blessed through you and your offspring" (28:14). Jacob argues this to Laban:

---

[4] Holladay, *Lexicon*, p. 235.
[5] Another possible translation is, "I have become rich and the Lord has blessed me...." (NIV margin), taking the verb as cognate with the Akkadian verb *naḥāšu*, "to flourish, prosper." Hamilton (*Genesis 18-50*, p. 282) prefers this, since he says divination purports to gives information about the future, not about the past.

"The little you had before I came has increased greatly, and the LORD has blessed you wherever I have been." (30:30)

Jacob asks that after the current striped or spotted sheep and goats are removed from the flock, he get all striped or spotted animals that are subsequently born. Thus, when Jacob is saying, "Don't give me anything" (30:31) he means, "Don't give me anything of the current huge flock; only those variegated animals that may be born in the future." In the Near East sheep are normally white and the goats are black. At most, the variegated animals might constitute 20%.[6]

Jacob seems to be settling for so little, thinks Laban. He agrees, smiles, and the same day removes all the abnormally colored sheep and goats, putting them in the care of his sons whom he sends three-day's journey away (30:36). Laban will fix him! But Laban hasn't reckoned with God.

Breeding Variegated Sheep and Goats (30:37-43)

Jacob, ever the entrepreneur, seeks to maximize the number of spotted and streaked goats and sheep by state-of-the-art breeding techniques: having the animals mate in front of brown and white striped sticks, on the theory that what they saw at conception would affect the embryo. It sounds like an old wives' tale. It certainly doesn't have any scientific basis. Did this superstition make Jacob rich? No. Not any more than mandrakes make a woman fertile (30:14-16). Yet God increases his flocks.

Laban, seeing how successful Jacob is becoming in developing larger and larger variegated flocks, begins changing the terms of the deal. Each time he does, God changes the coloration patterns of the kids and lambs being born.

As Jacob explains to Rachel and Leah,

> "... The God of my father has been with me.... Your father has cheated me by changing my wages ten times. However, God has not allowed him to harm me. If he said, 'The speckled ones will be your wages' then all the flocks gave birth to speckled young; and if he said, 'The streaked ones will be your wages,' then all the flocks bore streaked young. So God has taken away your father's livestock and has given them to me" (31:5-9).

Jacob is under no illusions. He has been diligent and has done all he knows to do, but he attributes the results to God. He knows that his peeled poplar sticks don't fine-tune the coloration patterns that Laban keeps changing. It has to be God himself!

---

[6] Hamilton, *Genesis 18-50*, p. 283.

3. Jacob and Laban, Rachel and Leah (Genesis 29-31)

Hundreds of years later, Moses exhorts the people of God never to forget God's role in wealth creation:

> "You may say to yourself, 'My power and the strength of my hands have produced this wealth for me.' But remember the LORD your God, for it is he who gives you the ability to produce wealth...." (Deuteronomy 8:17-18)

Q2. (Genesis 30:25-43) At what point do you think Jacob realizes that his breeding techniques are not the cause of his growing wealth? According to Deuteronomy 8:17-18, what danger are we in when our income and assets begin to increase?
http://www.joyfulheart.com/forums/index.php?showtopic=934

God Commands Jacob to Return to Canaan (31:1-13)

The more God blesses him, the more Jacob begins to feel uneasy. Laban's sons are complaining that Jacob is taking their father's wealth away from him and there is increasing tension with Laban (31:1-2). But more important than that by far, the Lord speaks directly to Jacob to return:

> "Go back to the land of your fathers and to your relatives, and I will be with you." (31:3)

Jacob calls his wives Rachel and Leah away from the encampment into the fields so he can talk to them privately and make his case for leaving. If Jacob is to escape with his family and new-found wealth, he needs the active, willing cooperation of his wives. They are on Laban's turf. If Laban decides to prevent them from leaving, he and the men he commands can keep them there by force or intimidation – and, if they escape at all, it will be only with what they can carry on their backs (31:42).

So Jacob shares with his wives about God's material blessings in spite of Laban's constantly changing terms (31:4-9). He recounts his vision of an angel of God and repeats Yahweh's specific words:

"I am the God of Bethel, where you anointed a pillar and where you made a vow to me. Now leave this land at once and go back to your native land." (31:13)

Rachel and Leah Back Jacob (31:14-16)

Rachel and Leah are united in what they should do. They feel used by their father: he has "sold" them and then used up the money.

Legally, a father is supposed to hold and use the bride price only for a time. Then the money, in whole or in part, is to revert to the daughter at such time her father dies or if she is impoverished by her husband's death.[7] But no money had changed hands – Jacob had traded seven years of labor for the bride in lieu of cash. Thus Rachel and Leah have no future whatsoever if they stay with their father.

They, too, feel Laban is resentful towards Jacob: "Does he not regard us as foreigners?" (31:15). They're ready to leave with Jacob.

Jacob's Family Escapes from Haran (31:17-21)

Once the decision is made, they await an opportune time. When Laban goes to shear the sheep, the time has come.

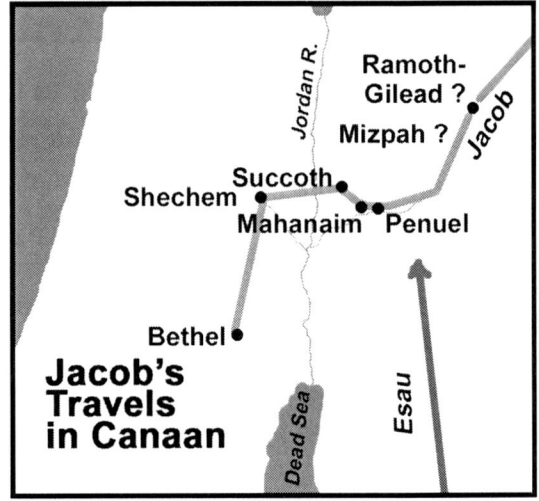

> "17 Then Jacob put his children and his wives on camels, 18 and he drove all his livestock ahead of him, along with all the goods he had accumulated in Paddan Aram, to go to his father Isaac in the land of Canaan.
>
> 19 When Laban had gone to shear his sheep, Rachel stole her father's household gods. 20 Moreover, Jacob deceived Laban the Aramean by not telling him he was running away. 21 So he fled with all he had, and crossing the River, he headed for[8] the hill country of Gilead." (31:17-21)

---

[7] Hamilton, *Genesis 18-50*, p. 289; Roland de Vaux, *Ancient Israel*, 1:26-29.
[8] "Headed for" (NIV) is literally, "set his face toward" (NRSV, KJV), denoting movement towards a specific location (Hamilton, *Genesis 18-50*, p. 291, fn. 8).

3. Jacob and Laban, Rachel and Leah (Genesis 29-31)

Laban Pursues Jacob (31:22-30)

When Laban is told "on the third day" (31:22), he gathers a large band of his relatives and takes off in hot pursuit. How *dare* they! It is one thing to grow large herds at his expense. It is even worse to leave before he had a chance to get them back! From Laban's reaction, it is pretty easy to see why Jacob, Rachel, and Leah – who knew him well – decided to leave unannounced. With his controlling attitude toward Jacob and his family, Laban would not have allowed them to leave if he could stop them.

But Laban "the Aramean" is accosted by God the night before he catches up with Jacob, in the hill country of Gilead, northeast of the Sea of Galilee.

> "Then God came to Laban the Aramean in a dream at night and said to him, 'Be careful not to say anything to Jacob, either good or bad.'" (31:24, cf. 29, 42)

In other words, Laban is forbidden "from threatening Jacob with any harm."[9]

Laban is still angry and complains how Jacob has deceived him and "carried off my daughters like captives in war." He claims he would have sent them away "with joy and singing to the music of tambourines and harps." I can see Jacob, Rachel, and Leah looking at one another trying to suppress a smile. They knew what Laban would have done.

Theft of Household Gods (31:30-35)

> "Rachel stole her father's household gods" (*terāpîm*, 31:19b)
>
> "[Laban asked] 'Why did you steal my gods (*'elōhîm*)?' .... Now Jacob did not know that Rachel had stolen them." (31:30, 32)

Laban levels a serious charge: stealing his household gods. These were *teraphim*, portable idols, small enough to conceal inside a camel's saddle. Of course, Rachel's monotheist descendants, who would later read this story, would laugh. How can you steal a god – a real god? Rachel is guilty of "god-napping."

Example of a small image from a later period, about 7 inches tall. Nude female figure (8th–7th century BC), Levant, Tell Duweir (Lachish), ceramic; 18.1 x 8.8 cm, Metropolitan Museum of Art, New York.

---

[9] Hamilton, *Genesis 18-50*, p. 299.

But why would she do this? One ancient tablet found at Nuzi seems to indicate that possession of the family gods constituted title to the chief inheritance portion and headship of the family.[10]

A simpler explanation, however, is that she steals them for protection on her journey to Canaan. She had been raised believing in their power. She isn't quite ready to replace her old way with Jacob's new faith – especially when threatened with the greatest change and challenge of her life. She is like many Christians, who have made some profession of faith, but haven't fully repented of some of their pagan ways – and in times of crisis fall back into what they know and trust.

Jacob knows nothing about Rachel's theft. He vows that anyone found with the gods will be killed. Rachel deliberately deceives her father and succeeds in keeping him from discovering the gods in his search of the tents.

But Jacob finds out. Years later, Jacob commands his household, "Get rid of the foreign gods you have with you and purify yourselves...." (35:2), when Jacob consecrates himself and family before God at Bethel.

Q3. (Genesis 31:17-36) Why did Jacob and his family leave without saying good-bye to Laban? In what sense did they "deceive" Laban? (31:20, 27). Was anything they did unjust or unrighteous? If so, how?
http://www.joyfulheart.com/forums/index.php?showtopic=935

The Covenant at Mizpah (31:36-55)

Jacob angrily confronts his father-in-law when Laban doesn't find any proof of the theft. He justifies himself. He took nothing that wasn't his. He had worked 14 years for Laban's daughters and another six years for the flocks that are now his.

---

[10] See the discussion in Hamilton, *Genesis 18-50*, p. 294.

3. Jacob and Laban, Rachel and Leah (Genesis 29-31)

> "If the God of my father ... had not been with me, you would surely have sent me away empty-handed. But God has seen my hardship and the toil of my hands, and last night he rebuked you." (31:42)

God has "rendered judgment"[11] against Laban and thus rebukes him.

Jacob has been discerning in his assessment of Laban's possessiveness, for immediately his father-in-law says,

> "The women are my daughters, the children are my children, and the flocks are my flocks. All you see is mine." (31:43)

Laban did not recognize Jacob's right to anything, but God has warned Laban sternly and Laban is afraid to take anything by force. So Laban calls for a covenant between them. Here are some of the elements of the covenant described in this passage:

- A stone **pillar** (31:45), such as Jacob had set up in Bethel.
- A heap of stones (31:46-49a) which they named Mizpah (watchtower) and Galeed or Gilead (**witness heap**).
- Calling on **Yahweh as witness and guarantor** of the covenant: "May the LORD keep watch between you and me...." (31:49b).
- A **promise** from Jacob not to mistreat his wives, nor to take rival wives to displace them from their status (31:50).
- A **non-aggression pact**: "I will not go past this heap to your side to harm you...." (31:51-52).
- An **oath** in the name of God (31:53).
- A sacrifice and **fellowship/covenant meal** together (31:54).

Notice, to whom Laban swears compared to Jacob:

Laban	Jacob
"the God of Abraham and the God of Nahor, the God of their father" (31:53a).	"the Fear of his father Isaac" (31:53b), literally, "the One of Isaac who inspires dread."[12]

---

[11] "Rebuked" (NIV, NRSV, KJV), "rendered judgment" (NASB) is *yākaḥ*. In the Niphal stem it can mean "argue out together (in legal dispute). Here in the Hiphil stem it means either "set someone right, reprove," or "give judgment" (Holladay, *Lexicon*, p. 134).

[12] Hamilton, *Genesis 18-50*, p. 310.

Does Jacob wonder whether the God of Nahor and Abraham's father Terah (11:26-32) was the true God? Is that why he swears by "the Fear of his father Isaac" instead? We don't know.

Many centuries later Joshua recounts,

> "Long ago your forefathers, including Terah the father of Abraham and Nahor, lived beyond the River and worshipped other gods." (Joshua 24:2)

It is possible that Jacob saw a distinction that Laban did not. Or it may have been just a way of reminding Laban that "the Dread of Isaac," who had appeared to Laban with a warning not to harm Jacob, would be watching to make sure he obeyed.

Mizpah Is Not a Sentimental Word at Parting

When I was a boy, I heard the Mizpah covenant said as a parting word between friends:

> "The LORD watch between me and thee, when we are absent one from another." (31:49, KJV)

But this was no sentimental saying. It was a threat with divine sanction that meant: If you break this covenant when I can't see you, may God watch you and punish you. The word "watch," ṣāpâ, "conveys the idea of being fully aware of a situation in order to gain some advantage or keep from being surprised by an enemy." *Mispeh* (from the verb ṣāpâ, "watch") means, "watchtower, lookout point."[13]

Q4. (Genesis 31:44-55) What are the terms of the Mizpah Covenant? Of what is the Mizpah monument supposed to remind Jacob and Laban?
http://www.joyfulheart.com/forums/index.php?showtopic=936

---

[13] John E. Hartley, ṣāpâ, TWOT #1950, 1950b.

3. Jacob and Laban, Rachel and Leah (Genesis 29-31)

The location of Mizpah is somewhere in the "hill country of Gilead" (NIV, NRSV), "mount Gilead" (KJV, 31:21, 24), north of the Jabbok River, perhaps near Rammoth-Gilead, on the main road, the "King's Highway" that ran from Damascus down to Elath at the tip of the Gulf of Aqaba.[14]

Blessing and Conflict

When you look at Jacob's sojourn in Haran, he has a lot to complain about.

- **Deceit**. He is tricked into an extra seven years of labor.
- **Idolatry**. He has at least one wife – his true love – who worships idols.
- **Family conflict**. There's an ongoing conflict between Jacob's wives and children.
- **In-law injustice**. Later he endures constant struggle with Laban who changes his wages ten times, always trying to better himself at Jacob's expense.
- **Escape**. He has to flee when Laban is away to be able to go home.

Do you call that blessing?

But look at it from a larger perspective. Jacob came empty-handed and left with many children and great wealth. Indeed, God has been with him and watched over him (28:14-15) – and even blessed Laban on his account (30:27).

Too often when we are experiencing trials we complain. "Nothing seems to be going right." How hard our life is. Too often we can't see the forest for the trees.

Blessing *always* comes amidst conflict. Name one person in the Bible whom God blessed and blessed others through, and I'll show you struggle and suffering. Sometimes we act as if God has "promised us a rose garden." He has promised to bless us and to be with us, but he doesn't promise all sunny skies. Jesus told his disciples:

> "I have told you these things, so that in me you may have peace. In this world you will have trouble. But take heart! I have overcome the world." (John 16:33)

---

[14] The Hebrew word is *har*, "mountain, hill, hill country"(*Har*, BDB p. 249). Mizpah is probably located either near Mt. Gilead, or on the mountain opposite Gilead (A.F. Rainey, "Mizpah," ISBE 3:387-388). Ramoth-Gilead is identified with Tell Rāmîh, near the present border between Syria and Jordan. The location is almost certainly on the main road south from Damascus (the King's Highway; William S. LaSor, "Ramoth-Gilead," ISBE 4:40-41).

And this is God's word to you today, you who feel defeated, beat up, and sorry for yourself. Jesus says to you: Take heart, don't be discouraged, my child. I have overcome the world.

Q5. Why do we often fail to see God's blessings during the everyday conflicts of our lives? Why do blessings and conflicts so often come at the same time? What hope do we have in the midst of our struggles?
http://www.joyfulheart.com/forums/index.php?showtopic=937

Prayer

Father, thank you for your promise that you will never leave us or forsake us. Help us to see your blessings and give you praise, even through our tears. In this crucible of life in which we are being purified, help us to bring glory to you. In Jesus' name, we pray. Amen.

4. Jacob Wrestles with God and Man (Genesis 32-33)

No sooner than Jacob is clear of the threat of Laban's armed band, than he hears news that is much more troubling. Jacob had sent messengers ahead to let his brother Esau know he is coming. They return with the report:

> "We went to your brother Esau, and now he is coming to meet you, and four hundred men with him." (32:6)

Laban had only suffered loss of property; Esau has been nurturing a murder wish against Jacob for twenty years! No wonder Jacob is in "great fear and distress" (32:7).

James J. Tissot, "Jacob Sees Esau Coming to Meet Him" (c. 1896-1902), gouache on board, 21.3 x 30 cm, Jewish Museum, New York.

Sign of the Angelic Army (32:1-2)

But knowing this was coming, God sends a wonderful sign to Jacob.

> "Jacob also went on his way, and the angels of God met him. When Jacob saw them, he said, 'This is the camp of God! So he named that place Mahanaim.'" (32:1-2)

In Bethel, Jacob had seen angels in his dream, ascending and descending a staircase to heaven and called the place Beth-el, "house of God" (28:17-19). Here he sees angels and exclaims, "This is the camp of God!" (32:2). God, who had promised him in Bethel to watch over him wherever he went (28:15), has not forgotten.

Jacob's small encampment of wives and children, servants and livestock, is matched by God's nearby encampment of an army of angels. When Jacob moves, the angelic army moves as well, shadowing him, protecting him from any harm. When Laban had gotten his band of men within range to threaten Jacob, God had spoken a stern warning

(31:24, 29, 42), and Laban had complied. Jacob realizes that his camp is protected by God's camp, so he names the place Mahanaim, in Hebrew "two camps."[1]

> Q1. (Genesis 32:1-2) Why does God reveal the angel army to Jacob? What is the significance of the presence of this army? Why do you think he calls the place Mahanaim ("two camps")?
> http://www.joyfulheart.com/forums/index.php?showtopic=938

Preparing to Meet Esau (32:3-21)

Jacob knows he must reconcile with Esau if he is to live in the land to which God has sent him, and so he makes careful preparations.

1. Jacob sends messengers ahead

First, Jacob sends messengers ahead so that he will not surprise Esau suddenly by word of his presence.

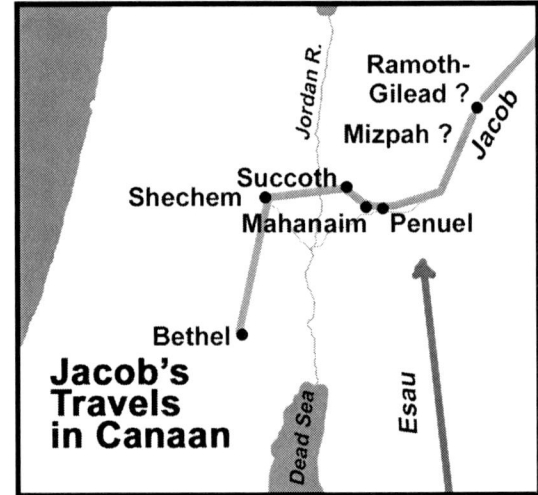

> "This is what you are to say to my master Esau: 'Your servant Jacob says, I have been staying with Laban and have remained there till now. I have cattle and donkeys, sheep and goats, menservants and maidservants. Now I am sending this message to my lord, that I may find favor in your eyes.'" (32:4-5)

The messengers are to bring several things to Esau's attention:

---

[1] Kidner, *Genesis* p. 167.

4. Jacob Wrestles with God and Man (Genesis 32-33)

- **Peaceful**. Jacob has been with their uncle Laban for 20 years and is only now returning home. Jacob shows that his past actions constitute no threat to Esau, and that he has not secretly returned home without Esau's knowledge to somehow gain further advantage over Esau.

- **Wealthy**. Jacob is wealthy and returns home with a considerable fortune. Thus he does not need what Esau has and poses no threat to Esau's goods. He does not need to exercise the birthright inheritance of double the inheritance Esau would receive. Jacob is independently wealthy. And he is not sneaking home, his tail between his legs. He comes on his own and is a person to be reckoned with.

- **Humble**. Jacob comes humbly. He instructs his servants to refer to Esau as his lord, his superior. All his life Jacob had been struggling to be Esau's lord. He had tricked Esau into handing over his birthright and had deceived in order to receive the blessing of the firstborn from his father. But now he comes acknowledging Esau as his lord. This may be the formal deference of courtesy, but it is deference nevertheless.

- **Healing**. Jacob comes to seek Esau's favor and heal the rift between them.

2. Jacob prays (32:9-12)

Next, Jacob prays.

Gustave Doré (1832-1883), "The Prayer of Jacob," engraving.

" ⁹O God of my father Abraham, God of my father Isaac, O LORD, who said to me, 'Go back to your country and your relatives, and I will make you prosper,' ¹⁰ I am unworthy of all the kindness and faithfulness you have shown your servant. I had only my staff when I crossed this Jordan, but now I have become two groups. ¹¹ Save me, I pray, from the hand of my brother Esau, for I am afraid he will come and attack me, and also the mothers with their children. ¹² But you have said, 'I will surely make you prosper and will make your descendants like the sand of the sea, which cannot be counted.'" (32:9-12)

Jacob reminds God that he is returning in obedience to God's own instructions. He acknowledges his own unworthiness of God's great blessings to him. We see both humility and thankfulness have grown in Jacob these twenty years since he first met God at Bethel.

Now he asks for God's salvation (rescue) and protection from Esau. He admits his fear for himself and for his wives and young children, all under 13 years of age. This kind of transparency in prayer is another indication that Jacob has gotten to know God. He concludes with a reminder of God's promise to him and his ancestors that God would prosper him and make him fruitful.

Does Jacob remind God of his promises as some kind of persuasive leverage? Perhaps. But we must understand that these promises are the bedrock of Jacob's own faith. He believes and has acted on God's instructions to return home. God has confirmed the blessings of Abraham to him, and he believes them, too. I think Jacob reminds God of his promises as a faith-statement. It is this faith that props Jacob up when he is afraid. He shares with his God both his fears and his faith, and so his prayer is an authentic, faith-filled prayer. How Jacob has grown!

Q2. (Genesis 32.9-12) What does Jacob's prayer tell us about his fears? About his faith? About his pride? What are the signs of spiritual growth you see in Jacob since he left Canaan to go to Haran years before?
http://www.joyfulheart.com/forums/index.php?showtopic=939

4. Jacob Wrestles with God and Man (Genesis 32-33)

3. Jacob prepares a succession of gifts to appease Esau (32:13-21)

Look at the quantity of animals he gives to Esau:

1.	200 female, and 20 male goats		220
2.	200 ewes and 20 rams		220
3.	30 female camels and their young		30
4.	40 cows and 10 bulls		50
5.	20 female donkeys and 10 male donkeys		30
		Total	550

Five hundred fifty animals, 490 of which are female and will cause Esau's herds to increase rapidly.

Jacob gives instructions that the animals are to be sent as individual groups, each with space between it and the next, so that the cumulative effect will be of one gift after another. Perhaps if Esau is angry when he encounters the first herd, his anger will have abated somewhat by the time the fifth herd reaches him. Each herder is to bring the same humble message when he meets Esau's army:

> "They belong to your servant Jacob. They are a gift sent to my lord Esau, and he is coming behind us." (32:18)

Jacob's purpose is clearly stated:

> "I will pacify him with these gifts I am sending on ahead; later, when I see him, perhaps he will receive me." (32:20)

Jacob seeks to pacify with generous gifts a tribal chieftain whom he has offended, much as centuries later, Abigail, the wife of churlish Nabal (who insulted David), seeks to pacify David with gifts and gracious words to David who is coming with his own 400 men (1 Samuel 25:18-31).

Jacob is traveling down the east side of the Jordan, southward in the direction of Seir, Esau's lands, in Edom. He has just come to the Jabbok ravine, a small river flowing into the Jordan from the east. Jacob has sent the herds of animals ahead of him the previous afternoon, but he stays the night on the banks of the Jabbok.

4. Jacob divides his party into two groups (32:7-8; 33:1-2)

Jacob's final preparation is to divide his party into two groups to avoid a wholesale massacre.

Wrestling with God (32:22-32)

At nightfall, Jacob sends his wives and children across the ford in the Jabbok River with all their possessions, ready for an early start in the morning. But he stays behind, as the Scripture records,

> "So Jacob was left alone, and a man wrestled with him till daybreak." (32:24)

Who is this strange antagonist? What is the significance of this struggle? While the event is shrouded by darkness and mystery, several things emerge as we meditate on it.

God the Wrestler

First, we find that the "man" is a manifestation of God himself. Hosea calls him both an "angel" and God:

> "In the womb he grasped his brother's heel;
> as a man he struggled with God.
> He struggled with the angel and overcame him;
> he wept and begged for his favor." (Hosea 12:3-4)

James J. Tissot, "Jacob Wrestles with an Angel" (c. 1896-1902), gouache on board, Jewish Museum, New York.

Would God reveal himself as a wrestler? Isn't God gentle and peaceful? Yes, and he is also just and holy and a God of vengeance. Both the Old and New Testaments give many indications of God's violent judgment upon the unrighteous. In his letters, Paul refers to spiritual conflict as "wrestling," both struggling with the dark powers, as well as struggling in prayer before God (Ephesians 6:12; Colossians 1:29; 2:1; 4:12).

Who is Jacob struggling with in the night? Is it with a ghost? A phantom? A river god guarding the ford of the Jabbok? A spirit who can only manifest itself in the darkness and must flee at dawn? All these pagan theories of Jacob's struggle ignore the text itself which clearly identifies the Wrestler as none other than God (32:28, 30).

4. Jacob Wrestles with God and Man (Genesis 32-33)

Symbolism and Reality

Was this a symbolic wrestling? In the daytime, we are often too busy to dwell on the past, but at night our worries often increase. Haven't you ever struggled with your conscience at night? Agonized over problems? Been buffeted with fears of the day to come? Jacob had elements of deceit and trickery in his past. In the morning he would face the consequences of them. He had little sleep the night before.

So it *is* symbolic, you cry. Yes, I would respond, it is *very* symbolic, but it was physical, too. One can't spiritualize away the injury to Jacob's hip socket, and the limp that characterized his walk in later years. These were not just symbols of his encounter and humbling before God, they were physical remnants of the struggle, too.

Sometimes we have trouble believing in events that we can't understand on the basis of our own experience. We have experienced the mental and spiritual anguish and struggle of the night, but not the physical, and so we doubt. This event is both physical *and* symbolic!

God's Testing

But having said that, I can't say I fully understand what was going on. Why couldn't the "man" (God) overpower Jacob? Certainly, God's strength is infinite. What is the significance of laming Jacob at the close of the conflict?

As a father, I've wrestled with my sons and daughter on the lawn or the living room floor. I've seen their intent expressions of maximum effort to best me, and I have resisted their strength to encourage persistence and greater effort, rather than always pinning them with my obviously superior strength. Cats play with their kits in mock battles to teach them and challenge them. This must have been some kind of testing of Jacob's persistence.

Sir Jacob Epstein, "Jacob and the Angel (1940-1941), alabaster, 7' h x 3' w. Tate Collections, London.

Unless You Bless Me (32:26)

Somehow, Jacob recognizes that this is no human assailant. This is a divine messenger who has the power to bless him. Jacob and the "man" are locked in combat, but are at an impasse. Neither can overcome the other, but neither wants to release his grip for fear that the other will take advantage of the moment. The "man" injures Jacob's hip, but still he holds on. The "man" finally says:

"Let me go, for it is daybreak."

Jacob is tenacious and persistent:

"I will not let you go unless you bless me."

Unless the "man" will speak words of peace and blessing to him, Jacob will not release him.

"What is your name?"

"Jacob,"

"Your name will no longer be Jacob [meaning 'supplanter'], but Israel [meaning 'he struggles with God'], because you have struggled with God and with men and have overcome" (32:27-28).

A New Name: Israel (32:28)

This new name from God is significant. We see several times throughout the Bible that a new name is a sign of a new place with God, a new phase of faith.

- Abram is renamed Abraham ("father of nations," 17:5)
- Sarai is renamed Sarah ("princess," 17:15)
- Simon is renamed Peter ("rock," Matthew 16:16-18)

One of the promises to people of overcoming faith in Revelation is "a new name … known only to him who receives it" (Revelation 2:17).

God, who has struggled with Jacob, now bestows on him a new name to remind all that he has "struggled with God and with men and have overcome" (32:28). Jacob's new name now contains the name of God *(-el)* within it. What a heritage: to be known as one who has met both God and man and succeeded! What a goal for us to strive for in our own spiritual pilgrimage!

Peniel – the Face of God (32:30)

Jacob now asks the "man's" name, but receives instead a question ("Why do you ask my name?") and a blessing in return. Centuries later Manoah, Sampson's father, asks an angel his name with a similar answer. "Why do you ask my name? for it is beyond your

4. Jacob Wrestles with God and Man (Genesis 32-33)

understanding" (KJV, Hebrew "wonderful"; Judges 13:17-18). Jacob receives the blessing and calls the name of the place Peniel (Hebrew, "face of God"), saying,

> "It is because I saw God face to face, and yet my life was spared." (32:30)

Jacob's Limp (32:31-32)

So at dawn's light, Jacob receives yet another blessing, and walks – no, limps – into what the day will hold between him and his brother Esau. I like this verse:

> "The sun rose above him as he passed Peniel, and he was limping because of his hip." (32:31)

Twenty years before, when Jacob met God, he had left Bethel a new man. Today, as well, Jacob departs from his encounter a changed man, a marked man.

Jacob's limp isn't so much a mark of discipline, but a remembrance of encounter – a mark which reminded him ever after of the seriousness with which he served his God, a mark of faith which he carried to his grave.

Q3. (Genesis 32:24-30) Who was the "man" Jacob wrestled with? What does the wrestling represent? Was it spiritual or physical? Why does the "man" wound Jacob permanently? What do you think the limp means to him?
http://www.joyfulheart.com/forums/index.php?showtopic=940

Jacob Meets Esau (33:1-16)

Jacob is struggling as he limps forward, pushing himself to walk in spite of the throbbing pain in his hip. Now out in front of his two parties of wives and children, he looks up and sees Esau "coming with his four hundred men." He goes forward bowing himself all the way to the ground seven times as he approaches his brother as a sign of obeisance to his brother. Esau runs to meet him, but instead of anger is an embrace, instead of thrusting a knife, he offers a kiss of peace. After a lifetime of enmity the two brothers are reconciled.

We will pass over the formalities quickly. The children and their mothers come bowing and are presented. "These are the children God has graciously given your servant," Jacob explains.

"⁸ Esau asked, 'What do you mean by all these droves I met?'

'To find favor in your eyes, my lord,' he said.

⁹ But Esau said, 'I already have plenty, my brother. Keep what you have for yourself.'

¹⁰ 'No, please!' said Jacob. 'If I have found favor in your eyes, accept this gift from me. For to see your face is like seeing the face of God, now that you have received me favorably. ¹¹ Please accept the present that was brought to you, for God has been gracious to me and I have all I need.'

And because Jacob insisted, Esau accepted it." (33:8-11)

It is vital that Esau accept Jacob's peace gifts to him. To accept them puts Esau under obligation to Jacob. Once he has received these gifts from his brother's hand he cannot righteously take up arms against him. That would be seen in his culture as a sinister act of betrayal.

Jacob insists. Esau refuses politely. Jacob persists, for, he explains, "God has been gracious² to me and I have all I need." Notice how God's grace figures centrally in Jacob's conversation with his brother. He is not attributing his family and children to his own shrewdness, but to God's graciousness. This is no longer the Supplanter, but the one who looks to God for his very life and safety.

James J. Tissot, "The Meeting of Esau and Jacob" (c. 1896-1902), gouache on board, 18.1 x 27.4 cm, Jewish Museum, New York.

Now Esau offers to accompany Jacob, or to leave some men with him to protect him. Whether this is an act of brotherly care for Jacob's safety or a way of exercising power over Jacob we can't be sure. But Jacob politely declines to have any of Esau's men with them. He needs his

---

² *Hānan*, "show favor" (BDB 109).

freedom. And he doesn't want to move his family to Seir under his brother's headship. So he suggests that he will "come to my lord in Seir," but doesn't specify a time.

"So that day Esau started on his way back to Seir." (33:16)

Esau departs, and so far as is recorded, they only meet again briefly at their father's burial (35:29).

> Q4. (Genesis 33:1-16) How has Esau changed since Jacob had gone to Haran? How has Jacob changed? How does the encounter demonstrate Jacob's "craftiness"? How does it demonstrate his faith? Can Jacob be humble and "crafty" at the same time?
> http://www.joyfulheart.com/forums/index.php?showtopic=941

Reflections on Jacob's Wrestling

The story of Jacob's wrestling with God on the banks of the Jabbok moves me. Our walk with God includes some quiet and uneventful times where we seldom see his active intervention (though we are often blind to his care over us). At these times it seems that we experience little spiritual growth. But at the crisis times we are pushed up against God with no place else to turn. We are called to steps of faith, and as we take those difficult steps, we can move to a new place in God.

Jacob is told directly, "Go back to the land of your fathers" and is feeling the pressure of Laban's resentment of him. Does he obey God and face the threat of his brother's blood vengeance, which has been hanging over him for two decades, or stay where he continues to be dominated by his unfair and increasingly hostile father-in-law? Too often we take the path which requires of us the least change, even though it may mean taking backward steps from what God would have for us. Taking steps of faith requires the willingness to endure change and the unknown, relying upon God's resources rather than our own comfortable place of security. Jacob, to his credit, doesn't argue, but obeys God in spite of his fears.

At the Jabbok this profound change comes to a climax. Jacob has been leaning heavily upon God throughout this journey. He has seen God turn aside Laban's hostile forces, and now he has called upon God to keep him safe from his brother Esau, according to God's promises. The time of prayer leads to a time of intense struggle in the dark hours of night.

Jesus Wrestled with His Father in the Garden

I think of Jesus' struggle with his Father in the Garden of Gethsemane (Luke 22:39-46).

> "Father, if you are willing, take this cup from me; yet not my will, but yours be done." (Luke 22:42)

This is Jesus' step of faith, if you will. He knows how to minister for the Father on earth. He speaks words of power and energy to convert men's souls. His voice and touch heal men's bodies, as well, and drive away demons who have been tormenting their souls. Jesus knows this ministry.

But he is praying in Gethsemane because he senses that it is time to fulfill God's ultimate call upon his life, to die on the cross, carrying upon him all the sins of the world. While that which is human in him shuns death, this is not about physical death. That which is holy in him is repulsed by sin, but within a few hours he will feel the crushing load, the ugly, filthiness of compounded human sin bearing down upon him, suffocating him and creating between him and his Holy Father a gulf, a separation for the first time in all eternity. The Father cannot embrace sin, but must punish it. And the Son must cry out in agony of soul,

> "My God, my God, why hast thou forsaken me?" (Matthew 27:45-50),

and then, in faith, commit his spirit into the Father's hands. Like Jacob, Jesus wrestled with his Father in the Garden. And like Jacob he came from that struggle intent upon doing the Father's will.

You, too, may be locked in a great struggle with God. You will not let go and neither will he. You are marked by the struggle, never to be the same – exhausted, and yet you continue: "I will not let you go, Father, until you bless me," you say in your earnestness, in your persistence. And he does bless you.

The crisis of faith passes and you are changed by it, marked by it, and perhaps limping because of it. But you can step forth from your encounter into a new place of intimacy and knowledge of your Father, a place where your faith becomes unbounded and unfettered, a place where you are now ready to walk, or limp, wherever he would lead you, because you know that He will walk with you. May you and I arise from our struggle of faith to a new Day in the Lord!

> "The sun rose above him as he passed Peniel, and he was limping because of his hip." (32:31)

Prayer

Father, I think I've felt what Jacob has felt. Thank you for your crucible of change that has changed me. Let me walk forth to the new day that you bring for me. In Jesus' name, I pray. Amen.

5. Jacob Returns to Bethel (Genesis 33:17-35:29)

Jacob has met two adversaries on this journey, his father-in-law Laban and his brother Esau, and God has protected him from both. But there are dangers in Canaan, too.

Living in Succoth (33:17)

The first place Jacob lives in Canaan after his return is on the east side of the Jordan, a location known as Succoth.

> "Jacob, however, went to Succoth, where he built a place for himself and made shelters for his livestock. That is why the place is called Succoth." (33:17)

James J. Tissot, "Seduction of Dinah, Daughter of Leah" (c. 1896-1902), gouache on board, Jewish Museum, New York.

The place name Succoth (*sūkkôt*, the plural of *sukkâ*, "booth") is so named because Jacob built shelters or booths for his livestock there. He also built a house, since he apparently planned to stay for a while. In fact, though this residence only takes one verse in the Bible, he probably lived there for several years. Dinah is a child of about seven when the family left Haran, but is perhaps 15 by the time of her abduction in Shechem.

Jacob Settles in Shechem (33:18-20)

Now, after several years, Jacob and his family move to Shechem, to the west of the Jordan in Canaan.

> "[18] After Jacob came from Paddan Aram, he arrived safely at the city of Shechem in Canaan and camped within sight of the city. [19] For a hundred pieces of silver, he bought from the sons of Hamor, the father of Shechem, the plot of ground where he pitched his tent." (33:18-19)

He is planning to stay here, too, as evidenced by the fact that he purchases the land he will live on. Shechem had been a stopping place for Jacob's grandfather, Abraham, as well.

5. Jacob Returns to Bethel (Genesis 33:17-35:29)

> "Abram traveled through the land as far as the site of the great tree of Moreh at Shechem.... The Lord appeared to Abram and said, 'To your offspring I will give this land.' So he built an altar there to the Lord, who had appeared to him." (12:6-7)

Like his forebear, Jacob builds an altar there:

> "There he set up an altar and called it El Elohe Israel." (33:20)

Jacob is going by a new name now – Israel – given by the Lord (32:28), so he names the altar "El Elohe Israel," which means "God (is) God of Israel," recalling Jacob's vow made in Bethel:

> "If God will be with me and will watch over me on this journey ... then the Lord will be my God." (28:20-21)

The Rape of Dinah (34:1-5)

Being so close to the city, it is natural for Jacob's children, now teenagers, to develop friends in town, and to go into town when they have finished their chores. Dinah often visits her friends in town, and more and more she catches the eye of Shechem, the son of Hamor, leader of the town. One day, Shechem follows his lusts, takes[1] her, and rapes[2] her. Yet, in spite of his violent act, he loves her and is eager to marry her. He tells his father, "Get me this girl as my wife," that is, arrange a marriage for me.

Word travels fast. It is distressing to see Jacob's reaction – silence.

> "When Jacob heard that his daughter Dinah had been defiled, his sons were in the fields with his livestock; so he kept quiet about it until they came home." (34:5)

Jacob keeps quiet about it, meaning he doesn't rush to find and help his daughter Dinah or to confront the young man or his father. Jacob is about 104 years old at this point and probably frail. He waits until his sons come home – probably out of fear of the Shechemites.

Jacob's Sons Deceive Shechem (34:6-24)

As soon as they hear the news, the boys rush home "filled with grief and fury." Shechem's father Hamor, leaves Dinah at Shechem's house (34:17, 26) and, with

---

[1] "Took" (NIV, KJV), "seized" (NRSV) is *lāqaḥ*, "take." The word, used over one thousand times in the Old Testament gets its nuance from the context. Here "lay hold of, seize" seems to be the connotation (Walter C. Kaiser, *lāqaḥ*, TWOT #1124).

[2] The rape consists of two words: *shākab*, "lie down (for sexual relations)" and *'ānâ*, "afflict, oppress, humble."

Shechem and his other sons, come out to Jacob's tent to seek terms for marriage between Shechem and Dinah. Hamor asks Jacob to name whatever he wants for a bride price. We read no answer from Jacob, only from his sons.

"We can't give our sister to a man who is not circumcised," they say. They insist that all the men of Shechem be circumcised for a marriage to take place. This might seem plausible. Even though the Shechemites didn't practice circumcision, they had, no doubt, heard of peoples who circumcised men prior to marriage.[3] Hamor and Shechem, as members of the leading family in the town, convince the other men to consent. But where is Jacob's voice in this? Silent.

Three days after the circumcisions, when all the men are sore, Simeon and Levi, two of Dinah's full brothers (children of Leah) – probably joined by their servants – attack the town surreptitiously, kill all the men, and retrieve their sister. Then the other brothers loot the houses and carry off the women and children as slaves.

Just before Jacob's death, in Jacob's blessing of his sons, we find that this terrible sin has become a curse to them:

> " [5] Simeon and Levi are brothers –
> their swords are weapons of violence.
> [6] Let me not enter their council,
> let me not join their assembly,
> for they have killed men in their anger
> and hamstrung oxen as they pleased.
> Cursed be their anger, so fierce,
> and their fury, so cruel!
> I will scatter them in Jacob
> and disperse them in Israel." (49:5-7)

Jacob Intervenes – Too Late (34:30-31)

Only now does Jacob speak – out of fear. His sons have broken the peace.

> "[30] Then Jacob said to Simeon and Levi, 'You have brought trouble on me by making me a stench to the Canaanites and Perizzites, the people living in this land. We are few in number, and if they join forces against me and attack me, I and my household will be destroyed.'

---

[3] Hamilton (*Genesis 18-50*, p. 363, fn. 363) cites Roland De Vaux (*Ancient Israel* 1:47), who notes that the Hebrew words for bridegroom, son-in-law, and father-in-law all derive from the root ḥin, which in Arabic means, "to circumcise."

³¹ But they replied, 'Should he have treated our sister like a prostitute?'" (34:30-31)

Jacob seems more concerned with peace than honor. Derek Kidner observes:

> "The appeaser and the avengers, mutually exasperated, and swayed respectively by fear and fury, were perhaps equidistant from true justice. They exemplify two perennial but sterile reactions to evil."[4]

What should Jacob have done? Probably he should have pressed a legal accusation before the elders of the town, contending that the young man Shechem must be punished. Under the Mosaic Law centuries later, such a crime would have been punishable by death (Deuteronomy 22:25), though we don't know what law would prevail in this town at the time. Would the town elders have consented to punish Shechem? We don't know. On the one hand, Shechem is the son of the leader, but on the other hand, Jacob is a wealthy man in his own right who has influence in the area.

Nevertheless, instead of taking Shechem to court, Jacob is silent. The result is that he allows his sons to take matters into their own hands and commit a horrible crime.

Q1. (Genesis 34) Why do you think Jacob is so silent after the rape of his daughter? What should he have done instead of being silent? What was right about the sons' reaction? What was wrong? What threat does the family now face if they stay in Shechem?
http://www.joyfulheart.com/forums/index.php?showtopic=942

The Dangers of Intermarriage

But let's look at the situation from another perspective for a moment. Let's say Jacob's family *had* reached an agreement with the people of Shechem and begun to intermarry. How long do you think Jacob's descendants would have retained their unique

---

[4] Kidner, *Genesis*, , p. 174.

understanding of Yahweh, the true God? Not long. Centuries later through Moses, God gave these commands to the Israelites:

> "And when you choose some of their daughters as wives for your sons and those daughters prostitute themselves to their gods, they will lead your sons to do the same." (Exodus 34:16)

> "Do not intermarry with them. Do not give your daughters to their sons or take their daughters for your sons, for they will turn your sons away from following me to serve other gods, and the LORD'S anger will burn against you and will quickly destroy you." (Deuteronomy 7:3-4)

After the Israelites conquered the land under Joshua, there was continual intermarriage with the Canaanites, the people of the land. Chief among the offenders was King Solomon.

> "King Solomon loved many foreign women besides Pharaoh's daughter – Moabites, Ammonites, Edomites, Sidonians and Hittites. They were from nations about which the LORD had told the Israelites, 'You must not intermarry with them, because they will surely turn your hearts after their gods.' Nevertheless, Solomon held fast to them in love. He had seven hundred wives of royal birth and three hundred concubines, and his wives led him astray.
>
> As Solomon grew old, his wives turned his heart after other gods, and his heart was not fully devoted to the LORD his God, as the heart of David his father had been. He followed Ashtoreth the goddess of the Sidonians, and Molech the detestable god of the Ammonites. So Solomon did evil in the eyes of the LORD; he did not follow the LORD completely, as David his father had done.
>
> On a hill east of Jerusalem, Solomon built a high place for Chemosh the detestable god of Moab, and for Molech the detestable god of the Ammonites. He did the same for all his foreign wives, who burned incense and offered sacrifices to their gods."
> (1 Kings 11:1-8)

Intermarriage was never a racial issue, but a religious one. The Jews were separatist and exclusivist because God intended them to be. If there had not been a continual emphasis on Israel's uniqueness and separateness (holiness), the faith God was trying to teach them would have dissipated rapidly through syncretism (the combination of different religions and religious practices).

The Time to Teach a Nation

It took many generations for God to teach his people. He began through Abraham, Isaac, and Jacob – and then through Moses and Joshua, through Samuel and David, through the prophets.

How long does it take to infuse an entire nation with a radical conviction about the One True God (monotheism), in sharp contrast with the degraded polytheism of their neighbors? God is preparing his people so he might reveal Christ to them and redeem them "when the time had fully come" (Galatians 4:4).

Intermarriage in the New Testament

We read the same command against intermarriage in the New Testament. Again, this is not racial but religious.

> "Do not be **yoked together** with unbelievers. For what do righteousness and wickedness have in common? Or what fellowship can light have with darkness?" (2 Corinthians 6:14)

> "A woman is bound to her husband as long as he lives. But if her husband dies, she is free to marry anyone she wishes, but **he must belong to the Lord**." (1 Corinthians 7:39)

If You Are Married to an Unbelieving Spouse

The New Testament forbids intermarriage with unbelievers. But what if you're already married to an unbelieving spouse? In the early church, that was the case with thousands of people, especially among the Gentiles.

There's no way you can undo the past, even if you've made mistakes when you knew better. So confess it to God and make the best of it. He can still bless you as you surrender your life to him now. And there is hope for your spouse, too. Here's what the Apostle Paul taught on the subject:

> "[12] To the rest I say this (I, not the Lord): If any brother has a wife who is not a believer and she is willing to live with him, he must not divorce her.

> [13] And if a woman has a husband who is not a believer and he is willing to live with her, she must not divorce him. [14] For the unbelieving husband has been sanctified through his wife, and the unbelieving wife has been sanctified through her believing husband. Otherwise your children would be unclean, but as it is, they are holy.

> ¹⁵ But if the unbeliever leaves, let him do so. A believing man or woman is not bound in such circumstances; God has called us to live in peace.
>
> ¹⁶ How do you know, wife, whether you will save your husband? Or, how do you know, husband, whether you will save your wife?" (1 Corinthians 7:12-16)

We've explored intermarriage in the Bible. Now let's go back to the story of Jacob and his sons and the rape of his daughter Dinah. Jacob seems too willing to compromise and his sons too willing to act out of anger. Which course, in this case, best accomplished God's will for Jacob's family? Probably that of his hot-headed sons. What would have happened if Jacob had just stood up and said, "No!" to the Shechemites on behalf of his family and refused to allow Dinah to marry Shechem? I wonder.

Q2. What happened when the Israelites disobeyed God and intermarried with the Canaanites? Why do you think God commanded them not to intermarry? Was this racial or spiritual or both? Why are Christians to marry "in the Lord"?
http://www.joyfulheart.com/forums/index.php?showtopic=943

A Call to Rededication (35:1-15)

At the crisis following the slaughter at Shechem, God intervenes:

> " Then God said to Jacob, 'Go up to Bethel and settle there, and build an altar there to God, who appeared to you when you were fleeing from your brother Esau.'" (35:1)

This isn't just an escape from the danger of staying in Shechem. This is a renewed invitation to faith. Jacob sees it as a call to holiness and separation, and so he commands his household and other servants to purify themselves.

> " ² Get rid of the foreign gods you have with you, and purify yourselves and change your clothes. ³ Then come, let us go up to Bethel, where I will build an altar to God, who answered me in the day of my distress and who has been with me wherever I have gone." (35:2-3)

Who would have foreign gods in Jacob's household? His beloved wife, Rachel, for one. She had stolen her father's household gods when they had fled from Haran years before (31:19). She had clung to the false gods of her family.

Jacob's clan now included dozens of wives and children captured from Shechem, all of whom had grown up believing in idols and amulets. Some became family slaves, no doubt. Others may have became wives for his sons – we don't know. But apparently some of the Shechemite women and children wore earrings and other jewelry which had religious symbols or connotations. When they left Shechem to go to the house of God (Beth-el), Jacob was determined that they make a clean break with idolatry and to lead his suddenly-expanded household to trust in the true God Yahweh and in him only.

> "⁴ So they gave Jacob all the foreign gods they had and the rings in their ears, and Jacob buried them under the oak at Shechem. ⁵ Then they set out, and the terror of God fell upon the towns all around them so that no one pursued them." (35:4-5)

I can hear echoes of Jacob's call to repentance in Joshua's challenge centuries later to the people of Israel:

> "Now fear the LORD and serve him with all faithfulness. Throw away the gods your forefathers worshiped beyond the River and in Egypt, and serve the LORD....
>
> Choose for yourselves this day whom you will serve, whether the gods your forefathers served beyond the River, or the gods of the Amorites, in whose land you are living. But as for me and my household, we will serve the LORD." (Joshua 24:14-15)

Washing Bodies and Clothes (35:2)

"Purify yourselves and change your clothes," Jacob commanded his household (35:2b). What do washing and putting on clean clothes have to do with spiritual preparation? To Jacob's family it meant that their father's God demanded cleanness and their best.

Before the covenant was ratified on Mount Sinai, the LORD instructed Moses,

> "Go to the people and consecrate them today and tomorrow. Have them wash their clothes and be ready by the third day...." (Exodus 19:10-11)

Throughout the Book of Leviticus, bathing and washing one's clothes were ways one cleansed oneself from impurity and uncleanness. We see the same symbol in the tabernacle:

> " [Moses] placed the basin between the Tent of Meeting and the altar and put water in it for washing, and Moses and Aaron and his sons used it to wash their hands and

feet. They washed whenever they entered the Tent of Meeting or approached the altar, as the Lord commanded Moses." (Exodus 40:30-32)

Water, of course, is a symbol of spiritual cleansing. In the New Testament, the water of baptism is seen as a way to express repentance and to find purity before God through cleansing from sins (Acts 22:16; 2:38; 1 Corinthians 6:11; Titus 3:5; Hebrews 10:22; 1 Peter 3:21).

The Washing of Repentance

Our old ways won't do. We must cleanse ourselves and come before the Lord in holiness.

I can almost hear someone remark:

> We cannot cleanse ourselves, only God can cleanse us. We are saved by the grace of God, not by works.

But repentance is a requirement of salvation, isn't it? When Peter's listeners were cut to the heart on the day of Pentecost and asked what they should do, he told them,

> "Repent and be baptized, every one of you, in the name of Jesus Christ for the forgiveness of your sins. And you will receive the gift of the Holy Spirit." (Acts 2:37-38)

Man's part is repentance and washing (baptism); God's part is sending his blessing of forgiveness, and that is the true grace.

Q3. (Genesis 35:1-5) Why does Jacob's household need spiritual renewal? Why is it important to get rid of foreign gods? What do washing and putting on clean clothes represent? What "foreign gods" do you need to throw away? In what ways do you need to repent and lead a new, clean life?
http://www.joyfulheart.com/forums/index.php?showtopic=944

Building the Altar at Bethel (35:6-7)

> "⁶ Jacob and all the people with him came to Luz (that is, Bethel) in the land of Canaan. ⁷ There he built an altar, and he called the place El Bethel, because it was there that God revealed himself to him when he was fleeing from his brother." (35:6-7)

Jacob calls his household to prepare themselves spiritually first. "Then come," he says, "let us go up to Bethel, where I will build an altar to God" (35:3). In Bethel, Jacob built the altar, no doubt with the assistance of his sons. With them he has fulfilled the vow he made decades before in this very spot. It is a time of renewal and closeness to God.

God Appears to Jacob Again (35:9-13)

The narrator inserts here a blessing that Jacob receives about this time:

> "After Jacob returned from Paddan Aram, God appeared to him again and blessed him." (35:9)

God confirms to him the name of Israel, which Jacob had first received at Peniel (32:28). Then God reaffirms to him the Blessing of Abraham that we studied in Lesson 2.

> "¹¹ And God said to him, 'I am God Almighty; be fruitful and increase in number. A nation and a community of nations will come from you, and kings will come from your body. ¹² The land I gave to Abraham and Isaac I also give to you, and I will give this land to your descendants after you.' ¹³ Then God went up from him at the place where he had talked with him." (35:11-13)

Look at the elements of this blessing:

1. "I am God Almighty" (*El Shaddai*, 35:11b).
2. "Be fruitful and increase in number" (35:11c).
3. "A nation and a community of nations will come from you, and kings will come from your body" (35:11d).
4. "The land I gave to Abraham and Isaac I also give to you, and I will give this land to your descendants after you" (35:12).

God identifies himself this time as God Almighty, *El Shaddai*, a title God used first when he revealed himself to Abraham (17:1), and repeats here, and in 43:14; 48:3; and

49:25. The name may be linked to the word for "destroy, overpower,"[5] but we can't be sure. However, "Almighty" is probably a good translation.

The command to "be fruitful and multiply" is reminiscent of God's first command to Adam and Eve (Genesis 1:28). The promises of a great people and the land are part of the blessing that Jacob's father and grandfather had received before him.

> Q4. (Genesis 35:9-15) Why do you think God appears to Jacob yet another time? What are the primary promises that God renews to Jacob?

Acts of Worship (35:14-15)

> "¹⁴ Jacob set up a stone pillar at the place where God had talked with him, and he poured out a drink offering on it; he also poured oil on it. ¹⁵ Jacob called the place where God had talked with him Bethel." (35:14-15)

Jacob responded this time as he had responded the first time God had appeared to him at Bethel ("house of God"). He commemorated the event by setting up a memorial stone to the LORD and anointing it. But here he performs another act of worship:

> "He poured out[6] a drink offering on it" (35:14b).

---

[5] Victor P. Hamilton, *shādad*, TWOT #2333. Also Hamilton, *Genesis, 1-17*, pp. 462-463. See also David W. Baker, "God, Names of," DOTP 361. This meaning is also suggested by the wordplay in Isaiah 13:6, "Wail, for the day of the LORD is near; it will come like destruction (*shōd*) from the Almighty (*shadday*). John I. Durham (*Exodus* (Word Biblical Commentary, Volume 3; Nelson, 1987), p. 76-77) acknowledges that the word meaning is uncertain but sees a strong case made by MacLaurin that "Shaddai's primary character is one of power and military prowess," and that for the Hebrews his "predominant characteristic was his covenant-making with men."

[6] The verbs for pouring sound similar -- *nāsak* is used for pouring the drink offering, *yāṣaq* is used for pouring the oil, "pour, pour out, cast (metal)." *Yāṣaq* used of pouring out of oil in various anointings, as well as figuratively, pouring out water on a thirsty land (Isaiah 44:3) and pouring out the Spirit (Joel 2:28) (Paul R. Gilchrist, *yāṣaq*, TWOT #897).

5. Jacob Returns to Bethel (Genesis 33:17-35:29)

This is the first time in Scripture that we see the drink offering or libation poured out before the Lord. But later, in the time of the tabernacle and temple, drink offerings were offered twice daily. For example:

> "With the first lamb offer a tenth of an ephah of fine flour mixed with a quarter of a hin[7] of oil from pressed olives, and a quarter of a hin of wine as a drink offering." (Exodus 29:40)

In the New Testament, the Apostle Paul likened his imprisonment and sufferings as "being poured out like a drink offering on the sacrifice and service coming from your faith" (Philippians 2:17).

Jacob never built a physical "house of God" on this site at Bethel. All he built was an altar and a pillar, and with them were the memories of a sacrifice – of a lamb, of oil, of wine – and especially of the presence and word of the Lord. It was a precious place to Jacob.

A Forgotten Vow?

Many sermons have been preached on "The Forgotten Vow," blaming Jacob for not immediately fulfilling his vow before the Lord at Bethel, but rather delaying it by years of sojourning in Succoth and Shechem.[8] Let's examine the evidence. Years before, Jacob had vowed before the Lord at Bethel:

> "**If** God will be with me and will watch over me on this journey I am taking and will give me food to eat and clothes to wear so that I return safely to my father's house, **then** the LORD will be my God and this stone that I have set up as a pillar will be God's house, and of all that you give me I will give you a tenth." (28:20-22)

In Haran, God had spoken to him:

> "I am the God of Bethel, where you anointed a pillar and where you made a vow to me. Now leave this land at once and go back to your native land." (31:13)

Only at the end of Jacob's sojourn in Shechem does God call him specifically to return to Bethel:

---

[7] A quarter of a hin was probably about 1-1/2 gallons of wine (Carl Philip Weber, *hîn*, TWOT #494).

[8] Kidner (*Genesis*, pp. 171-172) blames Jacob for disobedience in not returning sooner. Gordon J. Wenham ("Genesis," in *Eerdmans Bible Commentary*, James D. G. Dunn, John William Rogerson (editors) (Eerdmans, 2003), p. 62) says, "Promises were made to Jacob at Bethel, and Jacob made vows there. With the fulfillment of the promises Jacob is duty-bound to return to Bethel to fulfill his vows."

"Go up to Bethel and settle there, and build an altar there to God, who appeared to you when you were fleeing from your brother Esau." (35:1)

Is Jacob wrong for not fulfilling his vow sooner? Here's my view:

1. **Immediate obedience**. When God calls him in Haran to return "to your native land," Jacob obeys immediately. Not until chapter 35 does God specifically tell him to dwell in Bethel, and Jacob obeys immediately.

2. **Probable visits**. Probably, in the intervening time, Jacob has visited both his father Isaac in Beersheba and the site at Bethel where God had appeared to him. We aren't told in Scripture, but I find it hard to believe that he hadn't made both of these trips.

3. **Vows not mentioned**. When Jacob does move to Bethel, we aren't told that he is fulfilling his vows. When he built an altar in Succoth named "God, the God of Israel," he had fulfilled the part of the vow that Yahweh would be his God. How he fulfilled the part of his vow concerning making Bethel the house of God or tithing we just aren't told. Vow fulfillment isn't the context of the return to Bethel story.

4. **Silence of Scripture**. Scripture does not condemn Jacob for not "fulfilling his vow" sooner – only preachers and commentators do. Where Scripture withholds judgment, I believe we should also.

Four Heartaches

Chapter 35 records three deaths, and the sin of Reuben, Jacob's firstborn.

1. Deborah, Rebekah's nurse, dies near Bethel (35:8). This short mention tells us several things. First, Jacob had gone to his father Isaac's home soon after Jacob had returned from Haran. (35:27 does not necessarily occur immediately prior to Isaac's death.) That explains Deborah living with Jacob's family in Bethel. And while the account mentions Deborah's death, it does not record Rebekah's. Jacob's mother Rebekah must have died during the twenty years Jacob was in exile in Haran. He had missed being with her at her death.

2. Rachel, Jacob's beloved wife, dies in childbirth as the family is traveling south (35:16-20), perhaps on their way to visit Jacob's father Isaac in Hebron. Rachel is Jacob's first love, and now she dies bearing for Jacob her second son. As she dies, she names the boy Ben-Oni ("son of my trouble"), but Jacob renames him Benjamin ("son of my right

5. Jacob Returns to Bethel (Genesis 33:17-35:29)

hand"). Benjamin is the last child of his favorite wife – and the last son born to him that we know of. After Joseph is kidnapped, Jacob's "life is closely bound up with the boy's life" (44:30).

3. Reuben, the firstborn son, is found sleeping with Jacob's concubine Bilhah (35:22), clouding the firstborn's claim to be eventual leader of the clan. This was more than youthful passion, it was a direct insult to his father. We don't read what action Jacob took, if any, but Jacob's disappointment is clear in the prophecy he gives over Reuben just before Jacob's death:

> "Reuben, you are my firstborn,
> my might, the first sign of my strength,
> excelling in honor, excelling in power.
> Turbulent as the waters, you will no longer excel,
> for you went up onto your father's bed,
> onto my couch and defiled it." (49:3-4)

Q5. (Genesis 35:22) What is the significance of Reuben's sin? In what way does it go beyond a sexual sin? We're not told, but how do you think this affected the family dynamics? Extra credit: Reuben has acted dishonorably here. In what ways does Reuben act honorably in the future? (37:21-29; 42:22, 37)
http://www.joyfulheart.com/forums/index.php?showtopic=946

---

4. Isaac, Jacob's father, dies at the family home in Hebron at the ripe old age of 180.

> "He breathed his last and died and was gathered to his people, old and full of years." (35:29)

Isaac's death marks the end of an era. Certainly Isaac was a blessed man, to see God's promise of descendents begin to blossom, with 12 grandsons, as well as a number of granddaughters. Esau and Jacob together bury him, perhaps the last time they meet.

Talking with God

As I look at this passage, two elements stand out to me. First, Jacob's calling his family to repentance and rededication. Jacob has just "blown it" in handling his daughter's rape, yet he doesn't quit, but calls his family with him to prepare for a new place with God.

Second is the sense of intimacy surrounding God's appearance to Jacob. The language used to describe this appearance seems startling in its directness:

> "God appeared to him again and blessed him." (35:9)

After the appearance, the Bible records,

> "Then God went up from him at the place where he had talked with him." (35:13)

What a privilege to have God talk with you, to have him speak with *you* in particular! This is a privilege accorded to few in the Old Testament. But we who are part of the New Covenant are all intended to be recipients of this awesome audience with God. We have an access to God – a fact which is amazing.

> "Let us then approach the throne of grace with confidence, so that we may receive mercy and find grace to help us in our time of need." (Hebrews 4:16)

We also have been called to an intimate relationship with God through the presence of the Holy Spirit in our lives. The Spirit leads us and within us cries, "Abba, Father ... while the Spirit himself testifies with our spirit that we are God's children" (Romans 8:14-16). Through the Spirit "we have the mind of Christ" (1 Corinthians 2:16).

I encourage you to spend time with God often, daily. Walk with him on a walk and tell him your thoughts. Sing to him, pray to him, listen to him. I've found that God does *guide my thoughts* if I seek him. But very occasionally he will speak to my heart with such clarity that I know it is he. His words are usually short and to the point, but are so nourishing and helpful. They are like tent-pegs fixed in the ground, which anchor my tent on a windy day.

> "Then God went up from him at the place where he had talked with him." (35:13)

Talk to us, too, O Lord.

Prayer

Father, our failings and sins weigh on us. We, like Jacob, need to be visited afresh by you. Come to us again in your fullness. We put away our gods. We repent before you. Come, Lord Jesus. In your holy name, we pray. Amen.

6. Jacob's Depression, Fear, and Hope (Genesis 37-47)

The next phase of Jacob's life is a time of bereavement and fear, of sadness and a kind of fatalist attitude towards life. Jacob has largely retired, and his sons have taken over the day-to-day duties of caring for the flocks and herds. The true love of Jacob's life, Rachel, has died in childbirth, leaving only her young son Benjamin and teenager Joseph by which to remember her. Something about Jacob seems paralyzed by Rachel's death. Something has died within him, and he lives on only in the life of her children.

In this lesson we'll be covering a great deal of ground, skipping over the details of Esau (chapter 36), Judah and Tamar (chapter 38), and much of Joseph's life (chapters 39-45). But we'll be stopping to observe Jacob at various points, to seek to understand what is going on in him, and to see what God does about it.

James J. Tissot, "Jacob Mourns His Son Joseph" (c. 1896-1902), gouache on board, 18.7 x 14.3 cm, Jewish Museum, New York.

The Loss of Joseph (chapter 37)

Joseph is the apple of Jacob's eye. The young man is granted a kind of special status far above his older brothers, causing tremendous resentment among them. As a teenager, he is out tending the flocks with his half-brothers. When something doesn't go his way, or when they do something behind their father's back, Joseph is the tattletale – and their father believes Joseph (37:2).

The High Cost of Favoritism (37:3-4)

> "³ Now Israel loved Joseph more than any of his other sons, because he had been born to him in his old age; and he made a richly ornamented robe for him." (37:3)

In his grief, Jacob makes the serious error of displaying openly his preference for one son over another. Now that Rachel is gone, his love and attention shifts to her son.

On some special occasion, Jacob presents Joseph a special coat. The exact translation is difficult. The word "robe" is clear, but *passîm*, from *pas*, "flat (palm) of hand,"[1] is difficult to understand. Here are some of the attempts:

- "Richly ornamented robe" (NIV).
- "Coat of many colors" (KJV), based on the Septuagint and Vulgate translations.
- "Long robe with sleeves" (NRSV), taking *pas*, "palm," to indicate the robe's sleeves reached to the palm and to the soles (flat) of the feet, as Aquila's translation.

Hamilton's rendering "a long, colorful tunic"[2] is probably a good compromise. We're just not sure exactly what it looked like. In 2 Samuel 13:18, a garment so named was royal apparel. Whatever it was, it was special, far beyond what Jacob had given any of Joseph's brothers. Jacob may have sewn it himself, which made it doubly special.

> "When his brothers saw that their father loved him more than any of them, they hated him and could not speak a kind word to him." (37:4)

Jacob should have known better. His own father Isaac had made Esau his obvious favorite. He knew how it felt to be less loved. He had seen how this selective love had caused hatred and threats of violence in his own case. But Jacob continued in his selective love and sowed the seeds of murder in his own family also.

Joseph's Dreams (37:5-11)

Joseph was not only a tattletale. He was also a dreamer. He told his brothers of seeing their sheaves of grain in the field bowing down to his sheaf. Their hatred grew. Next he dreamed of the sun and moon and eleven stars bowing down to him. Jacob himself rebukes Joseph:

---

[1] BDB 1108.
[2] Hamilton, *Genesis 18-50*, p. 407.

> "What is this dream you had? Will your mother and I and your brothers actually come and bow down to the ground before you?" (37:10)

Though he rebukes his son, yet he keeps wondering: What does this mean?

Selling Joseph into Slavery (37:12-36)

The older sons had gone north to graze the flocks near Shechem, so Jacob sends Joseph to make sure all is well with them. When they see him coming, their hatred boils over:

> "When they saw him in the distance, and before he reached them, they plotted to kill him. 'Here comes that dreamer....'" (37:18-19)

Finally, they decide to dispose of him by selling him to a caravan of Ishmaelites, Midianites headed for Egypt.

They dip the beautiful coat in goat's blood and bring it to their father. "We found this," they say. "Look to see whether it's *your son's* robe" (37:32) They don't tell Jacob any lies. They don't have to. Jacob creates his own horrible story of his beloved son's death:

> "It is my son's robe! Some ferocious animal has devoured him. Joseph has surely been torn to pieces." (37:33)

Jacob's heart and mind seem to stop. The old patriarch is overcome with grief and loss.

> "³⁴ Then Jacob tore his clothes, put on sackcloth and mourned for his son many days. ³⁵ All his sons and daughters came to comfort him, but he refused to be comforted. 'No,' he said, 'in mourning will I go down to the grave to my son.' So his father wept for him." (37:34-35)

His grief is inconsolable. Jacob is broken in spirit. His sons' deed of bitterness has not only destroyed their hated brother, but also their father. In the unbearable weight of his sadness, only in his young son Benjamin does he find some comfort (42:38; 44:20, 30-31). Benjamin is the little bit of Rachel's memory that still endures.

> Q1. (Genesis 37:31-35) What does bringing the blood-stained robe to Jacob say about these sons' attitude toward their father? How does this loss affect Jacob? How do you think it affects his future behavior?
> http://www.joyfulheart.com/forums/index.php?showtopic=947

Joseph's Fortunes in Egypt (chapters 39-41)

The boy who was "too big for his britches," who was "king of the mountain" in his father's household is now a slave. But he rises quickly under God's blessing. He is sold as a slave to Pharaoh's captain of the guard and is promoted to manage Potiphar's entire estate. When the nobleman's wife tries to seduce him, his sense of honor and responsibility cause him to flee from her. When she accuses him of attempted rape, he is thrown into prison under her husband's jurisdiction, the prison in which Pharaoh's prisoners are confined.

James J. Tissot, "Joseph Interprets Pharaoh's Dream" (c. 1896-1902), gouache on board, 15.1 x 22.6 cm, Jewish Museum, New York.

Joseph's faithfulness and abilities cause him to gain the trust of the warden, who sets him over the whole prison, though he is still confined. When Pharaoh's cupbearer is thrown in prison for offending the king, Joseph interprets dreams that come to pass exactly as Joseph had predicted. Two years later, when Pharaoh is troubled by dreams, the cupbearer remembers Joseph and sends for him to help. Joseph tells Pharaoh:

"The seven fat cows in your dream are seven years of abundance, while the seven gaunt cows are seven years of famine. Let Pharaoh appoint a man to take a fifth of the seven abundant harvests and store them away in granaries so that the country may not starve during the seven years of famine." (41:29-34, paraphrase)

Pharaoh sees God's hand in the interpretation and appoints Joseph himself to the task. In a single day, Joseph moves from being prison trustee to second in command over all Egypt.

A Famine Sends Jacob's Sons to Egypt (41:1-34)

The years of plenty are a time of abundance, but when a drought grips the entire region, famine comes. In Canaan, the harvests are meager and Jacob can buy no food despite his wealth. Jacob's clan faces starvation and death.

> "When Jacob learned that there was grain in Egypt, he said to his sons, 'Why do you just keep looking at each other?' He continued, 'I have heard that there is grain in Egypt. Go down there and buy some for us, so that we may live and not die.'" (42:1-2)

Jacob may have been passive when Dinah had been raped, but he takes the lead now.

So ten of the brothers go to Egypt to buy grain, leaving young Benjamin at home with their father, "because he was afraid that harm might come to him" (42:4).

When the brothers arrive in Egypt, Joseph recognizes them. He questions them closely about his father and younger brother Benjamin. "You are spies!" he says. Then to test them, he demands that one remain as hostage until the youngest brother Benjamin is brought with them to prove their story. He detains Simeon in prison, and sends the others back home with sacks full of grain. But curiously, he returns each man's silver and has his servants bury it in each man's sack of grain.

When they reach home and begin to empty their sacks, the pouches of silver coin fall out. None returns home without his silver. The grain is theirs for free.

Fear, Blame, and Stubbornness (42:35-38)

> "When they and their father saw the money pouches, they were frightened. Their father Jacob said to them, 'You have deprived me of my children. Joseph is no more and Simeon is no more, and now you want to take Benjamin. Everything is against me!'" (42:35-36)

This is paranoia fed by depression. Jacob has experienced more loss than he can endure. His mother, his mother's nurse, his Rachel, his father, his beloved son Joseph have all been taken from him. Benjamin is all he feels he has left – and now he will be taken from him, too! Jacob turns to blaming his sons for all his woes.

"Everything is against me!" Have you ever been overtaken by depression? Has your heart ever been broken by loss, your world shattered by death? Your world suddenly shrinks to only you and what has meaning to you. At such times it seems like you against the world.

It is amazing that this story of the patriarch Jacob was not whitewashed as it was retold again and again until it was finally written down in the book of Genesis. You'd think that all the negatives about this legendary ancestor would be stricken from the record as the Israelites sought to glorify their past. But no, the character seems very real. Too real – if you've ever felt what Jacob is feeling, if you've ever been depressed.

Now this ruler in Egypt requires that Benjamin be brought before him.

> "Then Reuben said to his father, 'You may put both of my sons to death if I do not bring him back to you. Entrust him to my care, and I will bring him back.' But Jacob said, 'My son will not go down there with you; his brother is dead and he is the only one left. If harm comes to him on the journey you are taking, you will bring my gray head down to the grave in sorrow.'" (42:37-38)

The "only loved brother," Jacob *could* have said. His obvious favoritism must hurt the other brothers. Jacob is thinking only of himself and how this might affect him. He is consumed by self-pity.

Preparing for the Second Trip to Egypt (43:1-13)

But events have a way of forcing us to do what we've sworn we would never do. The famine continues unabated and the grain from their sacks is finally depleted.

"Go back and buy us a little more food," Jacob says to his sons.

"Don't you remember, Dad, what the man said. He won't give us food unless we bring our brother."

"Why did you tell him you even had another brother?" says Jacob in reproof. You can tell that this is just the flare-up of an argument that has continued periodically over the past year.

"The man questioned us closely about our family," replies Judah. "How did we know he would say, 'Bring your brother down here'?"

Their children are slowly starving and their father is quibbling about Benjamin. It is almost more than the sons can bear.

Now Judah offers to take personal responsibility for Benjamin. "I myself will guarantee his safety; you can hold me personally responsible for him."

Jacob finally relents. "If it must be, then do this...." He explains to them how to appease their enemy, much as he had once appeased his brother Esau. They prepare a pitiful gift, "a little balm and a little honey, some spices and myrrh, some pistachio nuts and almonds."

"Take double the amount of silver with you, for you must return the silver that was put back into your sacks," adds Jacob. It has been nearly a full year, we assume, since the first trip to Egypt for food. How would a busy administrator dealing with thousands of starving people remember that a few foreigners were sent off with their money still in its pouches? But Jacob the deceiver is changed. He may be depressed and overcome with loss, but he is now honest.

"Take your brother also and go back to the man at once." Now that his mind is made up, he is ready to execute the plan immediately. There is no time for dithering. If it must be done, it must be done at once.

Jacob's Prayer (43:14)

> "And may God Almighty grant you mercy before the man so that he will let your other brother and Benjamin come back with you." (43:14)

Here it is finally, a prayer to God Almighty, El Shaddai. Jacob has grieved and blamed, but now he turns to God for blessing. It is just a glimmer of hope through the gloom of bereavement, but it is a glimmer nevertheless.

"As for me, if I am bereaved, I am bereaved." Finally, Jacob is willing to let the world go on, even if he must suffer. His selfishness gives way to resignation and he sends the brothers on their way.

> Q2. (Genesis 42:35-43:14) What is Jacob's state of mind after the first trip to Egypt? If you were a psychologist, how would you diagnose him? What factors have paralyzed Jacob mentally and spiritually? Why do you think Jacob changed his mind about going again to secure grain?
> http://www.joyfulheart.com/forums/index.php?showtopic=948

Joseph Confronts His Brothers (43:15-44:34)

The brothers return to Egypt, and Joseph is moved to see his brother Benjamin. But he cannot show his feelings now. He must test his brothers once more. What will they do this time when their youngest brother, their father's new beloved son, is threatened? Have they changed? Have they finally repented of what they had done to him?

The brothers return the silver sent back with them on the first journey. They do the honest, right thing.

"It is all right," says Joseph. "Don't be afraid. Your God, the God of your father, has given you treasure in your sacks. I received your silver."

Simeon is released from prison, and the brothers are banqueted in Joseph's private quarters, and are then sent home with bags of grain. But Joseph's own silver cup is secretly placed in the mouth of Benjamin's bag and their pouches of silver returned again.

No sooner than they have left the city, they are stopped and searched. Have they taken the missing cup? The cup is found in Benjamin's sack and the boy is taken into custody to become a slave.

The brothers "tore their clothes." They themselves had sold Joseph into slavery, but now when Benjamin is taken into slavery, they are visibly moved.

Judah now goes up to Joseph to plead with him for Benjamin's life.

"If the boy is not with us when I go back to your servant my father, and if my father, whose life is closely bound up with the boy's life, sees the boy isn't there, he will die. Your servants will bring the gray head of our father down to the grave in sorrow." (44:30-31)

Judah offers his own life in exchange for the life of the boy.

"How can I go back to my father if the boy is not with me? No! Do not let me see the misery that would come upon my father." (44:34)

Joseph Makes Himself Known (45:1-24)

Joseph can bear it no longer. His brothers *have* changed. They care about their father. They care about their brother. He orders all his servants out of the room and begins to weep. "I am Joseph!" he tells his brothers. "Is my father really still alive?"

James J. Tissot, "Jacob Makes Himself Known to His Brothers" (c. 1896-1902), gouache on board, 22.4 x 29.1 cm, Jewish Museum, New York.

His brothers are terrified. Their brother, whom they had sold into slavery, now has them fully in his power and none can deliver them. They don't know what to do. They are speechless.

"Come here," says Joseph, and proceeds to reveal to them an astonishing insight into God's plan.

"Do not be angry with yourselves for selling me here, because it was to save lives that God sent me ahead of you.... God sent me ahead of you to preserve for you a remnant on earth and to save your lives by a great deliverance. So then, **it was not you who sent me here, but God.**" (45:5-8)

Seldom does a person see the big picture in his lifetime, but Joseph could see it. Ever since his brothers had appeared the year before seeking food to keep their families from starving, Joseph had begun to understand what God's real purpose was.

Here is the Blessing of Abraham again. This isn't for Egypt, though God cares for the Egyptians. This isn't for Joseph's sake; he has power enough. This is God's purpose: to raise up a people whom no one could number. Joseph's part is to keep them from starving and to provide a place for them to grow in number and flourish. **This isn't about Joseph at all, but about God fulfilling his purposes.**

What an amazing insight!

Joseph weeps in his brothers' arms and sends them home to fetch their father to come and live in the best part of Egypt, with the knowing words, "Don't quarrel on the way!" (45:24).

Q3. (Genesis 45:4-8) Contrast Jacob and Joseph. Jacob has suffered great loss. Joseph has suffered great injustice. Why is Jacob's vision so bleak, but Joseph's so broad? What have been their differing responses to fear? What insight has kept Joseph from being bitter towards his brothers?

http://www.joyfulheart.com/forums/index.php?showtopic=949

Jacob's Reassurance (45:25-46:27)

The jubilant brothers' caravan finally arrives at Jacob's camp. They shout:

"Joseph is still alive! In fact, he is ruler of all Egypt." (45:26)

Jacob is stunned. Joseph alive? Could he allow himself to even consider the possibility? It would hurt too much to open old wounds, if it were not true. Sometimes we get into a place of looking at the dark side of everything. We can't see God's blessings even when they stare us in the face.

"But it *is* true," his sons insist, and they tell him Joseph's words and show him the carts Joseph has sent to carry him back. A smile breaks out over his long-sad countenance and he laughs. The scripture says:

6. Jacob's Depression, Fear, and Hope (Genesis 37-47)

"The spirit of their father Jacob revived. And Israel said, 'I'm convinced! My son Joseph is still alive. I will go and see him before I die.'" (45:27-28)

The next days are busy with preparations for the journey. Belongings of a lifetime are packed. Numerous families are gathered and told they will be leaving behind all they have known. Herds are gathered, and the caravan of Jacob and sixty-six sons and grandsons, plus wives and daughters and servants, leaves and heads south.

Jacob Journeys to Egypt (chapter 46)

Jacob stops in Beersheba. Here his grandfather Abraham had sojourned and had called upon the name of the Lord, the Eternal God (21:33). Here the Lord had appeared to Jacob's father Isaac and confirmed to him the promises of Abraham. Here Isaac had built an altar and called on the name of the Lord and dug a well (26:23-25).

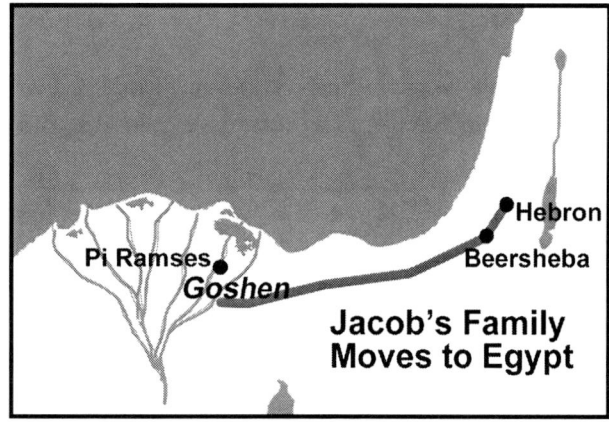

And now Jacob, on his way to see his son, stops in Beersheba and calls on the God of his father Isaac (46:1). He offers sacrifices, perhaps on the very altar Isaac had built many years before and is refreshed from the very well Isaac had dug.

That night God speaks to Jacob in a vision:

> "'Jacob! Jacob!'
> 'Here I am,' he replied.
> 'I am God, the God of your father,' he said. 'Do not be afraid to go down to Egypt, for I will make you into a great nation there. I will go down to Egypt with you, and I will surely bring you back again. And Joseph's own hand will close your eyes.'"
> (46:2-4)

When God speaks to us, all we can do is weep.

"Do not be afraid," God says. Jacob's life has been consumed by fear. Fear of Esau, fear of Laban, fear of Esau again, fear of the Canaanites after the destruction of Shechem. Fear of loss. Fear of loneliness. Fear. Fear has gripped him, and now God graciously releases him from its grasp. "Do not be afraid to go down to Egypt," he says.

Jacob has suffered loss after loss. His world has narrowed down until he clings to his youngest son Benjamin, only to have to give him up, too. He has nearly forgotten the promise of God to be with him.

"I will go down to Egypt with you," God promises him, "and will surely bring you back again."

So often we forget the companionship God offers, and turn to our own dwindling resources. There's an old hymn that expresses it well:

"O what peace we often forfeit, O what needless pain we bear,
All because we do not carry everything to God in prayer....

Are we weak and heavy laden, Cumbered with a load of care?
Precious Savior, still our refuge, take it to the Lord in prayer."[3]

Q4. (Genesis 46:2-4) Faith is what quiets our fears. What in God's word to Jacob at Beersheba quiets his fears? God had brought the same assurance to Jacob before (28:15; 31:3). Why do you think he had stopped believing it? What is the relationship between faith and God's words?
http://www.joyfulheart.com/forums/index.php?showtopic=950

And Joseph's Hand Will Close Your Eyes

Jacob has a future again. Like so many elderly people, his life had narrowed down to himself alone. Now his God will go with him. He will see Joseph and Joseph himself will be with him when he dies.

Jacob had left home the first time with nothing but a staff in his hand. This time when he leaves home, he counts a company of people as his descendants and household, including sixty-six sons and grandsons – a total of seventy when they are reunited with

---

[3] From the song "What a Friend We Have in Jesus," by Joseph M. Scriven (1855).

Joseph's family in Egypt – plus the wives and daughters and granddaughters and servants. Here is a man whom God has tried, but has also blessed – abundantly.

"Do not be afraid to go down to Egypt," or wherever your path is leading you, says your God, "for I will go down to Egypt with you and will surely bring you back again." Don't be afraid of your future. You have a Friend alongside.

Prayer

Father, so often, I've been afflicted with fear. At times in my life, it has gripped me in its evil fingers and motivated my decisions. Forgive me for not trusting in you. Forgive me for forgetting your promise to be with me. Father, I trust my future into your hands afresh. Thank you for your blessings of love and life and salvation in Jesus Christ. In His name, I pray. Amen.

7. Jacob Offers Blessings (Genesis 46:28-49:33)

The final phase of Jacob's life is one in which he is physically weak. But the depression that had haunted him for twenty years has now lifted. His spirit is soft again and we see the man of faith whom God had matured years before. Now, instead of focusing on his own pain, he is able to give to those around him once again. He becomes a conduit of the Lord's blessings.

A wagon carries old Jacob down to Egypt to his new home.

Benjamin West (1738-1820), "Jacob Blessing Ephraim and Manasseh" (1766-68), Allen Memorial Art Museum, Oberlin College, Ohio

"²⁸ᵇ When they arrived in the region of Goshen, ²⁹ Joseph had his chariot made ready and went to Goshen to meet his father Israel. As soon as Joseph appeared before him, he threw his arms around his father and wept for a long time. ³⁰ Israel said to Joseph, 'Now I am ready to die, since I have seen for myself that you are still alive.'" (46:28-30)

It is enlightening, though, that God's timetable for Jacob's death isn't the same as Jacob's. God still has work for him to do – blessing.

Blessing

We've seen the concept of blessing a number of times before:

- Isaac's blessing of Jacob and Esau (chapter 27)
- Isaac's blessing of Jacob when he leaves (28:1-5)
- The blessing of Abraham (28:4)
- The nations blessed through Jacob's offspring (28:14)

7. Jacob Offers Blessings (Genesis 46:28-49:33)

- Laban blessed through the presence of Jacob (30:27-28); Potiphar is blessed through the presence of Joseph (39:5)

One could argue that the whole story of the patriarchs – and Jacob in particular – centers around blessing: seeking a blessing, receiving a blessing, blessing others, and leaving a blessing as a legacy to one's descendents.

Blessing in the Bible

In Genesis and elsewhere in the Bible, spoken words have great import. We see in the Pentateuch, and Genesis especially, an understanding that blessing imparts something material as well as spiritual, in the same way as a curse prevents blessing.[1]

Irrevocable

A father conveys to his heir a blessing that is permanent and cannot be withdrawn, as in the case of Isaac being tricked into blessing Jacob. This idea is echoed elsewhere:

> Balaam: "See, I received a command to bless; he has blessed, and I cannot revoke it." (Numbers 23:20, NRSV)

> "As far as election is concerned, [the people of Israel] are loved on account of the patriarchs, for God's gifts and his call are irrevocable." (Romans 11:28-29)

From God

But a blessing is not just from the human father. It is from God. The blessing is a kind of spoken prayer or prophecy, since the one who possesses and dispenses all blessings is the Lord. In blessing Joseph, for example, Jacob says:

> "Because of your father's God, who helps you,
> because of **the Almighty,**
> **who blesses you** with blessings of the heavens above,
> blessings of the deep that lies below,
> blessings of the breast and womb." (49:25)

In a similar way, after the exodus, hundreds of years later, the Aaronic blessing was spoken by the priest, but conveyed by God.

> "The LORD said to Moses, 'Tell Aaron and his sons, "This is how you are to bless the Israelites. Say to them:

---

[1] Beyer (*eulogeō*, TDNT 2:754-755) discusses the concept of blessing in the Old Testament. See also, J. McKeown, "Blessings and Curses," DOTP, pp. 83-87.

> 'The LORD bless you and keep you;
> the LORD make his face shine upon you
> and be gracious to you;
> the LORD turn his face toward you
> and give you peace.'
>
> So **they will put my name** on the Israelites, and **I will bless them**."'" (Numbers 6:22-27)

The priest or father or prophet may speak the words that "puts my name" on the individual or people, but it is God who executes the blessing.

Often Conveyed by Laying on of Hands

In Genesis, the blessing is often conveyed by the laying on of hands (48:13-14, 17-19). Jesus blessed the little children by putting his hands on them (Matthew 10:16). When he imparted the blessing of healing to the sick, he usually laid his hands on them (Luke 4:40). One person might be blessed by the laying on of hands, but a multitude could be blessed by lifting up one's hands over them (Luke 24:50). The hands were used in blessing God as well. The gesture of lifting hands to God in prayer is found in the Old Testament, the New Testament – even in the Christian catacombs of Rome.[2]

A Kind of Inspired Prophecy

At Timothy's "ordination," the blessing was a prophecy conveyed by the laying on of hands by the elders:

> "Do not neglect your gift, which was given you through a prophetic message when the body of elders laid their hands on you." (1 Timothy 4:14)

In the Old Testament especially, curses are the opposite of blessings, kind of anti-blessings – spoken words that withhold blessing. The blessings and curses are often paired in the Pentateuch (Genesis 12:3; 27:12; 27:29; Numbers 22-24; Deuteronomy 11:26; chapter 30).

Though we don't have time to explore them at present, the concept of blessing in Genesis is closely related to promises, oaths, and covenants.

---

[2] See my article, "Lifting Hands in Worship," *Paraclete*, Winter 1986, pp. 4-8 (www.joyfulheart.com/scholar/hands.htm).

Joseph's Brothers Meet Pharaoh (46:31-47:12)

Along with Jacob, Joseph's brothers and their families arrive in Egypt and settle in Goshen.

Joseph now coaches his brothers on what to say to Pharaoh when they are introduced. Five of them are selected to represent the family before Pharaoh; Joseph wisely left the "loose cannons" at home (47:2). Or perhaps, when asking for hospitality for sojourners, he doesn't want to overwhelm Pharaoh with the whole clan of twelve brothers. Pharaoh might think twice about being so generous. Now Joseph coaches his brothers on how to present themselves:

> "³³ When Pharaoh calls you, and says, 'What is your occupation?' ³⁴ you shall say, 'Your servants have been keepers of livestock from our youth even until now, both we and our ancestors'— in order that you may settle in the land of Goshen, because all shepherds are abhorrent to the Egyptians." (46:33-34)

We're not exactly sure what Joseph means by this. Some scholars connect it with Egyptian history as a slur on the Hyksos rulers, Semitic invaders with Canaanite names, later termed "shepherd kings." But Joseph's reign probably fell within the Hyksos period (1720 to 1580 BC, if we adopt the earlier dating of the Exodus, which seems likely to me). Most likely the shepherd/livestock issue was related to class, that herding sheep was below the dignity of upper class Egyptians. Being an owner of livestock is different from being a shepherd, just like a rancher is considered a cut above a cowboy.

Though Joseph tells his brothers to describe themselves as "tenders of livestock" (46:34), they give their occupation as shepherds anyway. But Pharaoh doesn't seem to be alarmed (47:3). The family that had been characterized by deceit is now open about who they are, and God makes a way for them in spite of it. Pharaoh grants them freedom to live in Goshen (probably in the eastern part of the Nile delta near Tanis).

Jacob Blesses Pharaoh (47:7)

After Joseph's brothers leave the throne room, it is Jacob's turn.

> "Then Joseph brought in his father Jacob, and presented him before Pharaoh, and Jacob blessed Pharaoh." (47:7, NRSV)

Old Jacob is ushered slowly into Pharaoh's throne room. Suddenly the overpowering presence of the monarch seems to diminish as Jacob the patriarch is presented to him.

Jacob proceeds to bless Pharaoh. Usually, the greater would bless the lesser. But here, the man of God has much more to offer. He imparts a blessing to this king who has been so gracious to his family and has allowed them to sojourn in his lands. He fulfills the promise the Lord made to him years before: "Those who bless you be blessed" (27:29).

The Years of My Pilgrimage (47:8-9)

> "⁸ Pharaoh asked him, 'How old are you?'
> ⁹ And Jacob said to Pharaoh, 'The years of my pilgrimage are a hundred and thirty. My years have been few and difficult, and they do not equal the years of the pilgrimage of my fathers.'" (47:8-9)

The word "pilgrimage" (NIV, KJV) or "earthly sojourn" (NRSV) is *māgôr*, "dwelling, pilgrimage, place of sojourning, wherein one is a stranger," from the root *gûr*, "to live among people who are not blood relatives." Rather than enjoying native civil rights, the *ger* was dependent upon the hospitality of his hosts.[3]

Jacob views life as a temporary abode, a place of sojourning, not permanent residence. Many centuries later the writer of Hebrews echoes this thought. He says about the patriarchs:

> "They admitted that they were **aliens and strangers on earth**. People who say such things show that they are looking for a country of their own. If they had been thinking of the country they had left, they would have had opportunity to return. Instead, they were **longing for a better country** – a heavenly one. Therefore God is not ashamed to be called their God, for he has prepared for them a city." (Hebrews 11:13-16)

The Mindset of a Sojourner

The mindset of a sojourner is a vitally important perspective for Christians. During Jesus' ministry, this was his lifestyle and that of his disciples. He told one would-be follower:

> "Foxes have holes, and birds of the air have nests; but the Son of Man has nowhere to lay his head." (Luke 9:58)

We get so attached to our homes, to our communities, to our culture, to our comfortable way of life, that we have rejected the lifestyle of a sojourner for that of a permanent resident. But having a sojourner attitude is vital to discipleship; it steels us against strong temptations to conformity.

---

[3] Harold G. Stigers, *gûr*, TWOT #330c.

7. Jacob Offers Blessings (Genesis 46:28-49:33)

"Dear friends, I urge you, as aliens and strangers in the world, to abstain from sinful desires, which war against your soul." (1 Peter 2:11)

An old gospel song carries the same theme. It's a bit other-worldly in focus – but then again, that's what "longing for a better country – a heavenly one" means:

"This world is not my home, I'm just a-passing through.
My treasures are laid up somewhere beyond the blue.
The angels beckon me from heaven's open door
And I can't feel at home in this world anymore."[4]

> Q1. (Genesis 47:9) In what sense is life on earth like a "pilgrimage" or a journey with no permanent home? What happens to us when we settle down and get too comfortable with our lives? How do we retain a "journeying spirit" in our faith?
> http://www.joyfulheart.com/forums/index.php?showtopic=951

Old Age in the Era of the Patriarchs

We think that 130 is pretty old, but Jacob is not exaggerating when he says his years do not equal the years of his ancestors.

Nahor	119 years	(11:24)
Terah	205 years	(11:32)
Abraham	175 years	(25:7)
Isaac	180 years	(35:28)
Jacob	147 years	(47:28)
Joseph	110 years	(50:22)

I am sometimes asked, "Did they have another calendar?" Yes, they had a lunar calendar, but they still kept track of years by the changing seasons. It's pretty hard to mistake the passage of one year. So why did they live so long back then? We don't know. It may have had to do with the quality of the environment or the peacefulness of

---

[4] "This World is Not My Home" first appeared in a songbook in *Joyful Meeting in Glory No. 1*, edited by Bertha Davis (published 1919, C. Miller of Mt. Sterling, KY). It has since appeared in books by both Albert E. Brumley (1939) and J.R. Baxter (1946), but they are not the authors.

their nomadic lifestyle. Many Egyptian texts cite 110 years as the ideal life span, so long life among the Hebrews wasn't the exception. Later, though the ideal life span in Israel is somewhat less:

> "The days of our years are threescore years and ten;
> and if by reason of strength they be fourscore years,
> yet is their strength labor and sorrow;
> for it is soon cut off, and we fly away." (Psalm 90:10, KJV)

The contrast in Pharaoh's court couldn't have been greater. Jacob is a wizened old man, hunched over, shriveled, but still entirely in command of his senses. He shares his life with Pharaoh, leader of one of the most powerful countries in the entire world.

And then the interview is over.

"Then Jacob blessed Pharaoh, and went out from the presence of Pharaoh." (47:10)

The man of God conveys God's double blessing to the man of the world – on the way in *and* on the way out! It is the model of Jesus, who blessed wherever he went. What a model for us: to convey a blessing to those we meet!

Extracting an Oath from Joseph (47:29-31)

> "²⁷ Thus Israel settled in the land of Egypt, in the region of Goshen; and they gained possessions in it, and were fruitful and multiplied exceedingly. ²⁸ Jacob lived in the land of Egypt seventeen years; so the days of Jacob, the years of his life, were one hundred forty-seven years." (47:27-28)

In spite of the blessings of this new home, Jacob's heart is in the Promised Land. God has promised Jacob that "I will go down to Egypt with you, and I will surely bring you back again" (46:4). That return is on his mind.

James J. Tissot, "Jacob's Body Is Taken to Canaan" (c. 1896-1902), gouache on board, 17.4 x 26.9, Jewish Museum, New York.

> "²⁹ When the time drew near for Israel to die, he called for his son Joseph and said to him, 'If I have found favor in your eyes, put your hand under my thigh and promise that you will show me kindness and faithfulness. Do not bury me in Egypt, ³⁰ but when I rest with my fathers, carry me out of Egypt and bury me where they are buried.'
>
> 'I will do as you say,' he said.

7. Jacob Offers Blessings (Genesis 46:28-49:33)

³¹ 'Swear to me,' he said.

Then Joseph swore to him, and Israel worshiped as he leaned on the top of his staff." (47:29-31)

Jacob is failing. He calls for Joseph and makes him promise to carry his body for burial in the family burial place in Canaan.

Joseph promises, but Jacob insists, "Swear to me."

Placing one's hand under another's thigh (Hebrew *yārēk*) was a way of taking a solemn oath, which we saw when Abraham required an oath from his servant who was sent to Haran to get a wife for Isaac (24:9). "Thigh" seems to be a euphemism for the genitals. For example, Jacob's "direct descendants" in 46:26 are literally those who "came out of his loins," using the same word.[5]

After Jacob's death, Joseph goes to Pharaoh and says, "My father made me swear an oath" (50:5) and Pharaoh allows him to leave the country to fulfill his vow and bury his father in Canaan.

The scene closes with worship. The verb is *ḥāwâ*, "bow down deeply, do obeisance" in worship. It has the basic idea of to prostrate oneself on the ground, perhaps with the forehead to the ground as the Muslims pray.[6]

"Then Israel bowed in worship at the head of the bed." [7] (NASB)

Centuries later we see a similar posture from the dying David:

"And the king bowed in worship on his bed." (1 Kings 1:47, NIV)

---

[5] John E. Hartley, *yārēk*, TWOT #916a. The same word is used of Jacob's hip which was dislocated by the angel (32:25).

[6] "Worship" is the Histafal stem (Holladay, 97a) or perhaps the Eshtaphal stem (Edwin Yamauchi, *ḥāwâ*, TWOT #619) of *ḥāwâ*, "to prostrate oneself, to worship." It is cognate with the Ugaritic *ḥwy* "to bow down."

[7] In our passage there is a question about the appropriate translation. "Bed" is *miṭṭâ*. However, the Greek Septuagint, Syriac, and Vetus Itala translations (followed by the NIV) render this as "staff" (*maṭṭeh*). Hebrew was originally written with consonants only, with the vowels assumed by the context. Modern Hebrew, too, excludes vowels. But a group of Rabbinic scholars, the Masoretes of Tiberias, who sought to preserve the original pronunciation of the scriptures, added vowel pointing to the Hebrew text in perhaps the seventh century AD, producing the Masoretic Hebrew text of the Old Testament still used today. This fixed the meaning of any pronunciations – and word meanings – in question for those using this standard text. "Staff" (*maṭṭeh*) was the interpretation by the translators of the Greek Septuagint in the second century BC. "Bed" (*miṭṭâ*) was the interpretation of the Masorete scholars in the seventh century AD. Which is correct? God only knows for sure. To me a dying man bowing in worship at the head of his bed makes more sense that bowing at the head of a staff.

Jacob worships as he realizes that God will fulfill his promise through Joseph. God's promise of the land is important to him, even though it is only for now his final resting-place. For Jacob, to be buried in Canaan is to enjoy the firstfruits of the everlasting covenant.

Blessing Ephraim and Manasseh (48:1-20)

"¹ Some time later Joseph was told, 'Your father is ill.' So he took his two sons Manasseh and Ephraim along with him. ² When Jacob was told, 'Your son Joseph has come to you,' Israel rallied his strength and sat up on the bed." (48:1-2)

Jacob begins reciting his testimony and the Blessings of Abraham:

"God Almighty (*El Shaddai*) appeared to me at Luz in the Land of Canaan, and there he blessed me and said to me, 'I am going to make you fruitful and will increase your numbers. I will make you a community of peoples, and I will give this land as an everlasting possession to your descendants after you.'" (48:3-4)

Joseph's sons have heard these things, no doubt, from their father. But there's nothing like the impression of hearing in person a 147-year-old man tell you what God has done for him. These boys, who have been raised by the daughter of an Egyptian priest (41:50), need to hear the story of their faith again. Jacob tells again in their hearing the old, old story of the promises made to Abraham that are now being fulfilled.

These boys, who had never seen the Land, who had not known they were part of a larger family, were some of those promised descendants. They heard their grandfather's testimony and never forgot, but passed it on to their grandchildren after them. The ministry of a grandfather or a grandmother to their children's children should never be underestimated.

We read no plea from Joseph, but rather a special blessing from Jacob:

"Your two sons born to you in Egypt before I came to you here will be reckoned as mine; Ephraim and Manasseh will be mine, just as Reuben and Simeon are mine." (48:5)

In the Near East, the firstborn was to receive a double portion of the father's inheritance, with each of the other sons receiving a single portion. This helped insure that the firstborn would have the wealth and prominence to be the leader of the family. In this scene of blessing, Jacob is declaring that instead of Joseph getting a single share of Jacob's inheritance, that he will receive a double inheritance; Ephraim and Manasseh are to be considered Jacob's sons. Centuries later, when the people of Israel finally came into the Promised Land, the descendents of Ephraim and Manasseh receive their own separate lands in which to settle (Joshua 16-17).

Later we read about Jacob's firstborn son Reuben:

> "He was the firstborn, but when he defiled his father's marriage bed, his rights as firstborn were given to the sons of Joseph son of Israel; so he could not be listed in the genealogical record in accordance with his birthright, and though Judah was the strongest of his brothers and a ruler came from him, the rights of the firstborn belonged to Joseph." (1 Chronicles 5:1-2)

When he had been young, Jacob had deceived in order to gain his father's blessing. Now he is the patriarch giving the blessing. He is nearly blind (48:10) as was his father Isaac. But instead of being dulled spiritually by the smell of venison, he is spiritually acute.

Now old Jacob tells the story of the death of his beloved Rachel (48:7) and seems to drift off for a moment. Then he looks up, sees the boys, and asks, "Who are these?"

If you've ever been around an elderly parent, you know what's going on. The slippery memory that can recall events of long ago, sometimes has trouble with the present.

"These are the sons God has given me here in Egypt," says Joseph patiently.

"Bring them to me so I may bless them," says Jacob, still sitting on his bed. He embraces them and kisses them, though he can barely see them.

"I never expected to see you again," he says to their father, "and now God has allowed me to see your children, too." I can see tears on the cheeks of both father and son.

Joseph now bows himself on the floor before his father, as his sons look on. Is it worship? No, but honor and obedience. The boys watch as the Second in Command of all Egypt prostrates himself before an elderly shepherd who listens to God's voice. Now Joseph rises and brings the boys to Jacob for a blessing.

Prophetic Blessings

Joseph arranges his sons so that Joseph's firstborn, Manasseh, is next to Jacob's right hand, the preferred hand ("at his right hand"), while the younger Ephraim is on Jacob's left (48:13).

Mosan Workshop, Workshop of Godefroid de Huy (Netherlandish), "Jacob Blessing Ephraim and Manasseh" (mid-12th century), champlevé enamel on copper with gilding, 7.1 x 9.7 x 0.3 cm, The Walters Art Museum, Baltimore.

> "But Israel reached out his right hand and put it on Ephraim's head, though he was the younger, and crossing his arms, he put his left hand on Manasseh's head, even though Manasseh was the firstborn." (48:14)

Joseph is "displeased." This isn't going the way he wants it to happen. Surely his aged father is confused. He takes his father's right hand to move it from younger Ephraim's head to firstborn Manasseh's head (48:17-18) and to correct his father. One must do these things properly! Old Jacob tenses his arms and refuses to let Joseph move them, and when he speaks, he speaks in a conciliatory way to his favorite son:

> "'I know, my son, I know. He too will become a people, and he too will become great. Nevertheless, his younger brother will be greater than he, and his descendants will become a group of nations' ... so he put Ephraim ahead of Manasseh." (48:19-20)

What's going on here? How does Jacob know? He has heard from God and is doing what God is showing him to do. Though we aren't told anywhere that the Spirit of God is upon him, that is surely what is happening. He is prophesying God's words, just as his father Isaac had "mistakenly" prophesied the correct blessing over Jacob instead of Esau. Chapter 49 is a chapter of prophetic blessings over each of Jacob's twelve sons. If we understand these patriarchal blessings in any lesser way, we miss what is happening here.

Here he blesses the boys (48:16) with

1. Being called by his own name and the names of his father and grandfather,
2. Great increase in numbers, and
3. With legendary prosperity: "May God make you like Ephraim and Manasseh" (48:20).

Verse 22 is significant for two reasons. Jacob says to Joseph:

> "And to you, as one who is over your brothers, I give the ridge of land I took from the Amorites with my sword and my bow." (48:22)

First, it confirms that Joseph is over his brothers. Reuben had forfeited the birthright, and Joseph, the firstborn of Rachel, now holds it: he is over his brothers.

Second, he gives to Joseph "the ridge of land" he owns in Canaan. Where is this? When did this happen? We're really not sure, but this may be a reference to Jacob's sons' taking of Shechem in Genesis 34.[8]

Q2. (Genesis 48) Why does Jacob cross his hands when blessing Ephraim and Manasseh? Why does Joseph try to stop him? In what sense are Jacob's blessings an actual prophecy from God?
http://www.joyfulheart.com/forums/index.php?showtopic=952

Blessing of Jacob's Twelve Sons (49:1-28)

Now Jacob calls for his sons, sensing he is near death, and the twelve of them form around his bed.

"Gather around," says Jacob in a weak but audible voice, "so I can tell you what will happen to you in days to come" (49:1). He is clearly prophesying.

---

[8] Even though Jacob strongly disapproved of his sons' actions (49:5-7), nevertheless, in a sense their violent taking of the city certainly was seen as Jacob's act by the people of the land (34:30). He had purchased land outside Shechem from the owners, and then taken the entire area by the sword through the violence of Simeon and Levi. This is one attempt at an explanation, but no one really knows for sure what this verse means.

1. Reuben (49:3-4). Reuben, the firstborn, began well, but lost his birthright and place of honor as a result of incest with Jacob's concubine. Though we read of no immediate punishment at the time when the sin occurred (35:22), yet the sin had broad consequences, not only for Reuben but also for his descendents.

2 and 3. Simeon and Levi. Their anger and cruelty in the slaughter at Shechem becomes their legacy and they are "scattered."[9] The tribe of Simeon is eventually integrated into the tribe of Judah. The tribe of Levi is never given land of their own, but are given cities to live in, scattered throughout the land of Israel. Their inheritance is the tithe rather than land (Numbers 18:22-23).

4. Judah. The most extensive prophecies involve Judah and Joseph, the two leaders among the brothers, and the sons whose tribes, Judah and Ephraim, are destined to be the dominant tribes in the Promised Land. Ephraim in the north, eventually breaks off to become the Northern Kingdom and falls into idolatry and final exile to Assyria. The Southern Kingdom, Judah, sees periods of apostasy and revival, exile to Babylon and final return to rebuild the temple.

Judah is characterized as a lion's cub, a lioness who crouches, "who dares to rouse him?" He is powerful and a tribe to be reckoned with. In the first book of the Bible, Judah's tribe is symbolized by a lion. In the last book of the Bible we read of Judah's offspring:

> "See, the Lion of the tribe of Judah, the Root of David, has triumphed." (Revelation 5:5)

Most significantly, we read in vs. 10:

> "The scepter will not depart from Judah,
> nor the ruler's staff from between his feet,
> until he comes to whom it belongs,
> and the obedience of the nations is his." (49:10)

The KJV and NASB translate the third line, "until Shiloh come," following the Hebrew Masoretic text. However, there is good reason to render it "until he comes to whom it belongs" (NIV, RSV, following the Syriac and Septuagint translations with some Targums). Victor P. Hamilton notes: "This line has provoked more difference of opinion among Hebraists than perhaps any other in the entire book of Genesis."[10] He translates it, "until he possesses that which belongs to him." The sense seems to be that

---

[9] *Pāṣaṣ*, "be dispersed, scattered" (Victor P. Hamilton, TWOT #1745).
[10] Hamilton, *Genesis 18-50*, p. 654f, fn. 12.

the kingship will remain in Judah's clan until the King comes who can rightfully claim it. We Christians believe this to be Jesus the Messiah.

5. Zebulun,
6. Issachar,
7. Dan,
8. Gad,
9. Asher, and
10. Naphtali
   are each described very tersely.

11. Joseph, however, has the longest prophecy. We see images of fruitful vines, steady bows:

> "Because of the Mighty One of Jacob,
> because of the Shepherd, the Rock of Israel,
> because of your father's God, who helps you,
> because of the Almighty (*Shaddai*) who blesses you...." (49:24-25)

Blessings are from heaven and the deep, from the breast and the womb, greater than the ancient mountains.

> "Your father's blessings...
> Let all these rest on the head of Joseph,
> on the brow of the prince among his brothers." (49:26)

The final verse acknowledges Joseph as the leader and the firstborn among his brothers.

12. Benjamin receives the final blessing.

Jacob Dies (49:33)

Then Jacob gives final instructions concerning his burial place in the tomb Abraham had purchased centuries before (49:29-32):

> "When Jacob had finished giving instructions to his sons, he drew his feet up into the bed, breathed his last, and was gathered to his people." (49:33)

He, who has been blessed by God, has now finished blessing Pharaoh, his grandsons, and his twelve sons who are with him at the end.

Difficult Years Have Brought Jacob to God

Two verses in these closing chapters touch me especially. The first is this: Jacob tells Pharaoh,

"My years have been few and difficult." (47:9)

While we might disagree that they are few, we can agree that they have been difficult. Jacob has lived through the seasons of life. He has felt plenty of fear, mostly from family members – Esau and Laban. He has experienced the highs of love with Rachel and the depths of despair without her. Within a short time he lost his mother's nurse, his own dear wife, his father Isaac, and his son Joseph (to a violent death, he believed). He has learned to trust God to bless him, and his fortune has grown from a single staff in his hand (32:10) to great wealth, with hundreds of descendants who call him father, grandfather, and great-grandfather at his passing.

He has been overwhelmed by success and stunned into helplessness by life's blows. More than anything, however, his life is about God.

God met him at Bethel and promised to be with him, and there he vowed to serve God and tithe all that God gave him. He wrestled with God at Peniel and came away stronger in spirit for the contest, and ever after walked with a limp. He heard God's reassuring voice again at Beersheba after years of depression and despair,

"Do not be afraid. I will go down to Egypt with you, and I will surely bring you back again." (46:3-4)

Q3. Why do we equate blessing with a lack of crisis in our lives? What are the effects of crises on our faith? How do they help us grow in our faith? Why do they sometimes destroy our faith?
http://www.joyfulheart.com/forums/index.php?showtopic=953

God Who Has Been My Shepherd

In his blessing of Joseph and his sons (48:15-16) we can see Jacob's heart. He loves God; that is clear. He has known God now for the past 100 years – ever since Bethel –

and God has never let him down. As second phrase keeps echoing in my mind. When he blesses Ephraim and Manasseh he refers to

"The God who has been my Shepherd all my life to this day." (48:15b)

Jacob has spent his whole life as a shepherd. He knows how to breed them, to find them food, to protect them, and to guide them.

When I was in Israel in 1997, driving up the Jordan Valley towards Galilee, I saw a Palestinian shepherd with his sheep walking along the side of a hill. The shepherd was leading his sheep rather than herding them. He walked before them and they followed him, secure in his presence, protected from injury and harm. They didn't know where he was going, but that didn't matter. They trusted that he knew where *he* was going, and that was enough. They simply followed.

Your life has seen some ups and downs as well. You've seen the good and the bad, and it may be that today, as you read these words, you don't know the next step. The way is dark ahead, and you are afraid.

Do You Know the Shepherd?

I want to ask you a question: Do you know the Shepherd? I'm not asking if you know *about him*, but if you *know him*. The Shepherd that spoke to Jacob and guided him four millennia ago is still here and cares about each of his sheep. Specifically, he cares about you.

Some sheep are in his fold, safe, protected from danger, and well-fed. Others are straying on the hills, vulnerable, stumbling blindly, hoping to find their way in the dark, afraid.

Jesus told a parable about the man who has a hundred sheep and one of them wanders away. You leave the ninety-nine, he says, and go looking for the lost sheep until you find it. And when you find it, you joyfully put it on your shoulders and head for home. You call your friends and neighbors together to rejoice over finding the lost sheep. Jesus said,

"I tell you that there will be more rejoicing in heaven over one sinner who repents than over ninety-nine righteous persons who do not need to repent." (Luke 15:7)

The Shepherd is still searching the hills looking for lost sheep. He's searching, calling. That Shepherd is calling for you, listening for you, so you won't be lost any longer, but be found and rescued and safe.

You can help him in the search by uttering a simple phrase. "I'm over here, Lord. Help me." That's all you need to do – bleat – and he'll do the rest. Do it now. He's looking for you.

As he is dying, Jacob the old shepherd prays for two of his grandsons. "God who has been my Shepherd all my life to this day," he says, "may he bless these boys."

Q4. (Genesis 48:15) How did God act as a Shepherd to Jacob? How does God act as a Shepherd to you? Do you trust him or rebel against his shepherding?
http://www.joyfulheart.com/forums/index.php?showtopic=954

Prayer

Father, thank you for your presence, your love, your faithfulness to me. You have been with me in my greatest moments and in my deepest despair. Thank you for being with me. I pray for the person who has just completed studying these lessons. I pray that you will help him or her to reach out to you, and to invite you to be a personal Shepherd. Thank you, Lord, for being my Shepherd all my life. In Jesus' name, I pray. Amen.

Appendix - Participant Handouts

If you're working with a class or small group, feel free to duplicate the following handouts in this appendix at no additional charge. If you'd like to print 8-1/2" x 11" sheets, you can download the free Participant Guide handout sheets at: **www.jesuswalk.com/jacob/jacob-lesson-handouts.pdf**

Each of these lesson sheets includes:

Discussion Questions

You'll find 4 to 5 questions for each lesson. Each question may include several sub-questions. These are designed to get group members engaged in discussion of the key points of the passage. If you're running short of time, feel free to skip questions or portions of questions.

Lessons

Introduction

1. **Jacob the Deceiver** (Genesis 25:19-34; 27:1-41)
2. **Jacob Meets God** (Genesis 27:41-28:22)
3. **Jacob and Laban, Rachel and Leah** (Genesis 29-31)
4. **Jacob Wrestles with God and Man** (Genesis 32-33)
5. **Jacob Returns to Bethel** (Genesis 33:17-35:29)
6. **Jacob's Depression, Fear, and Hope** (Genesis 37-47)
7. **Jacob Offers Blessings** (Genesis 46:28-49:33)

Introduction to the Life of Jacob

Timeline

Approximate dates in Jacob's life following the "early dating" of the Exodus:

Date	Event	Genesis
2006 BC	Birth of Jacob and Esau, probably in Beer-lahai-roi	25:26
1966	Marriage of Esau in Beersheba, age 40	26:34
1930	Jacob's journey to Haran, age 76	28:2
1923	Jacob's marriages, age 83, Haran	29:23, 28
1918	Birth of Judah, Jacob's age 88	29:35
1916	End of Jacob's 14 year labor for his wives, Jacob's age 90	29:30
1916	Birth of Joseph	30:23
1910	End of Jacob's stay with Laban, age 96	31:41
1910	Jacob's arrival at Shechem	33:18
1902	Rape of Dinah	34:1-2
1900	Marriage of Judah, Judah is 18, Jacob is 106	38:1-2
1899	Selling of Joseph, Joseph is 17, Jacob is 107	37:2, 27
1888	Joseph imprisoned	39:20; cf. 41:1
1886	Joseph released from prison, made ruler of Egypt	41:1, 46
1886	Death of Isaac, Isaac is 180, Jacob is 120	35:28
1879	Beginning of famine, Jacob is 127	41:54
1878	Brothers' first visit to Egypt	42:1-2
1877	Brothers' second visit to Egypt	43:1; 45:6, 11
1876	Jacob's descent to Egypt at age 130	46:6; cf. 47:9
1859	Death of Jacob at age 147	47:28
1806	Death of Joseph at age 110	50:22

Copyright © 2010, Ralph F. Wilson <pastor@joyfulheart.com>. All rights reserved. Permission is granted to make one set of these participant handouts for each member of a local group or class at no charge.

Chief Places Jacob Lived

Beer-lahai-roi, Jacob's birthplace (25:11) means, "well of the Living One who sees me" (16:7). It is the site of a well in the Negev desert south of Beersheba, on the road to Shur, between Kadesh and Bered (16:14).

Beersheba, where Jacob lived as a boy, was the site of another well in the northern Negev desert. The name means "well of seven." It contains rich alluvial soil where crops could be grown and herds could be grazed. The region was controlled by Gerar, the nearest commercial center.

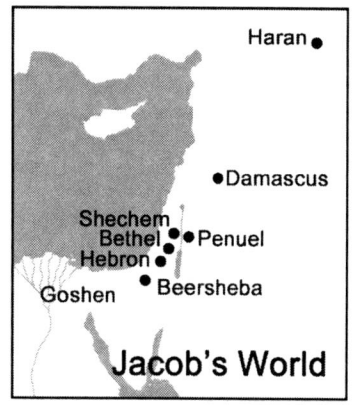

Gerar was a town in the western Negev desert, near Gaza, apparently controlled by Philistine or sea tribes during the patriarchal period (26:1, 8). Isaac and Jacob spent some time in Gerar (26:1) during their desert wanderings.

Haran, where Jacob labored for 20 years and raised his family, was the ancestral homeland of Jacob's ancestors. It is in present-day Turkey along the Jullab River.

Succoth, near where the Jabbok River enters the Jordan, was named after the booths (*sukkâ*) that Jacob built there for his livestock after reconciling with Easu and returning to Canaan (33:17).

Shechem is an ancient walled city that guarded the pass between Mount Ebal and Mount Gerizim, on the main road from Jerusalem to the north. Jacob's family camped on land outside the city near the Tree of Moreh (33:18).

Bethel is where God first appeared to Jacob (28:10-22) and where he returned later with his family (35:6). Originally named Luz, Jacob renamed it Beth-el ("house of God"). It lies on the main north-south watershed route about 12 miles north of Jerusalem.

Hebron (meaning "league" or "confederacy"), lies about 19 miles south of Jerusalem, close to the Tree of Mamre. It was an occasional home for Jacob (37:14) and the final residence of Isaac (35:27). At Sarah's death, Abraham had purchased a burial cave at nearby Machpelah from Ephron the Hittite (23:1-20). Abraham, Isaac, and Jacob and other family members were buried there (35:27-29; 47:30; 49:30; 50:13).

Goshen is a district in Egypt where Jacob lived the last 18 years of his life. The Israelites lived here until the Exodus centuries later in an area known as the "district of Ramases" (47:6, 11), probably near Pi-Ramases.

1. Jacob the Deceiver (Genesis 25:19-34; 27:1-41)

Q1. Why does the New Testament condemn Esau for selling his birthright? (Hebrews 12:16-17) What did selling the birthright represent? What does this transaction say about Esau's character and values? What does it reveal about Jacob's character and values?

Q2. Was Rebekah a spiritual woman, that is, interested in spiritual things? Was Isaac a spiritual man? Which do you think was the more spiritually sensitive? What evidence of spirituality do you see in Jacob? In Esau?

Q3. (Genesis 27:6-29) God had told Rebekah that Jacob is supposed to rule over Esau (Genesis 25:23). To what extent does this excuse her plan to deceive her husband Isaac? How much responsibility does Jacob bear in the deception?

Q4. (Genesis 27:33) Why couldn't Isaac reverse his blessing once he discovers Jacob's trickery? What is Isaac's role in this blessing? What is God's role in it?

Q5. (Genesis 25:28) What happens when your children sense that you love one child more than another? Did such discrimination happen to you when you were growing up? If so, how are you finding healing? How can we as parents love our children equally but differently?

Q6. Extra Credit. Whose character flaws most remind you of your own? Isaac's, Rebekah's, Esau's, or Jacob's? Why? How is God working to improve your character?

Copyright © 2010, Ralph F. Wilson <pastor@joyfulheart.com>. All rights reserved. Permission is granted to make one set of these participant handouts for each member of a local group or class at no charge.

2. Jacob Meets God (Genesis 27:41-28:22)

The Blessing of Abraham

1. **Fruitfulness** – numerous descendants,
2. **Land** – the land of Canaan, and
3. **World** – the nations of the world will be blessed.

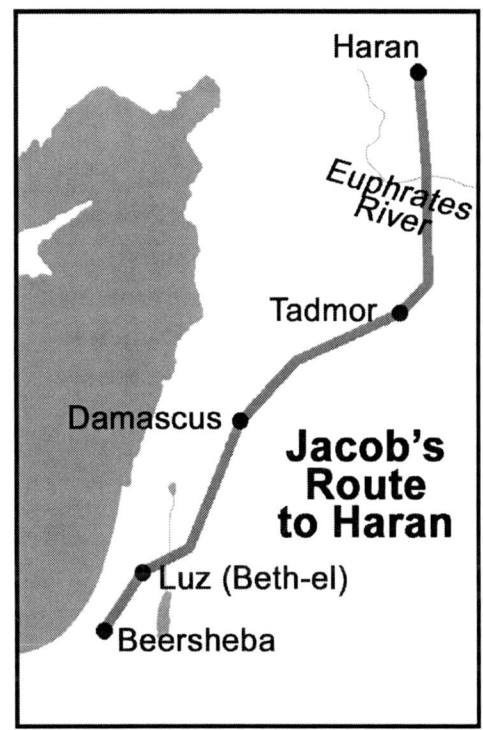

Q1. (Genesis 28:3-4) Why does Isaac bless Jacob, especially after Jacob's deception? How does this blessing compare to other blessings of Abraham, Isaac, and Jacob? What are the main elements of Isaac's blessing?

Q2. (Genesis 28:12-15) What did Jacob's dream of the angels ascending and descending from heaven signify to Jacob? What did God's blessing mean to him? In what way was this a conversion experience for him?

Q3. (Genesis 28:18-21) What did it mean to Jacob to set up the stone? What did anointing the stone mean to him? Why does he do these things? What does he promise God in his vow?

Q4. (Genesis 28:22) What does Jacob's promise to tithe indicate about his commitment? Presumably, Jacob has been a believer in Yahweh all his life. In what sense is this incident at Bethel a conversion experience for him? What is the relationship of tithing to conversion?

Copyright © 2010, Ralph F. Wilson <pastor@joyfulheart.com>. All rights reserved. Permission is granted to make one set of these participant handouts for each member of a local group or class at no charge.

3. Jacob and Laban, Rachel and Leah (Genesis 29-31)

Q1. (Genesis 29) Why do you think God allows Jacob to be tricked into 14 years of labor for two wives? What purposes do you think God is working out through these circumstances?

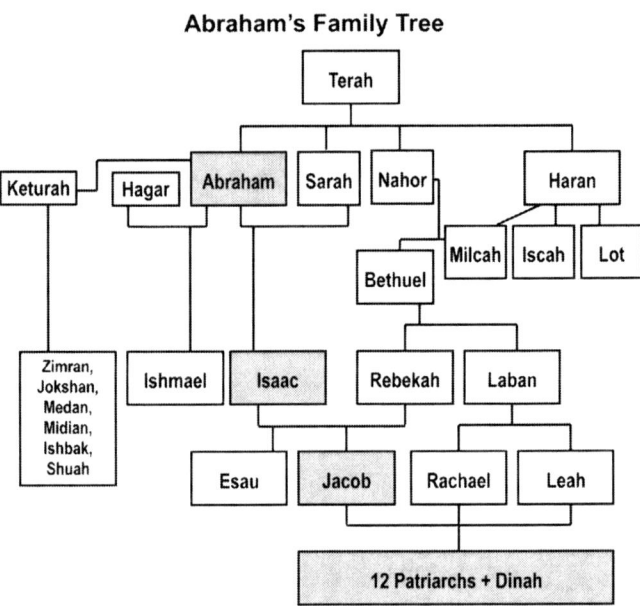

Q2. (Genesis 30:25-43) At what point do you think Jacob realizes that his breeding techniques are not the cause of his growing wealth? According to Deuteronomy 8:17-18, what danger are we in when our income and assets begin to increase?

	Name	Meaning	Mother
1.	Reuben	"see, a son"	Leah
2.	Simeon	"one who hears"	Leah
3.	Levi	"attached"	Leah
4.	Judah	"praise"	Leah
5.	Dan	"he has vindicated"	Bilhah
6.	Naphtali	"my struggle"	Bilhah
7.	Gad	"good fortune" or "a troop"	Zilpah
8.	Asher	"happy"	Zilpah
9.	Issachar	"reward"	Leah
10.	Zebulun	"honor"	Leah
11.	Joseph	"may he add"	Rachel
12.	Benjamin	"son of my right hand" (35:18)	Rachel

Copyright © 2010, Ralph F. Wilson <pastor@joyfulheart.com>. All rights reserved. Permission is granted to make one set of these participant handouts for each member of a local group or class at no charge.

Q3. (Genesis 31:17-36) Why did Jacob and his family leave without saying good-bye to Laban? In what sense did they "deceive" Laban? (31:20, 27) Was anything they did unjust or unrighteous? If so, how?

Q4. (Genesis 31:44-55) What are the terms of the Mizpah Covenant? Of what is the Mizpah monument supposed to remind Jacob and Laban?

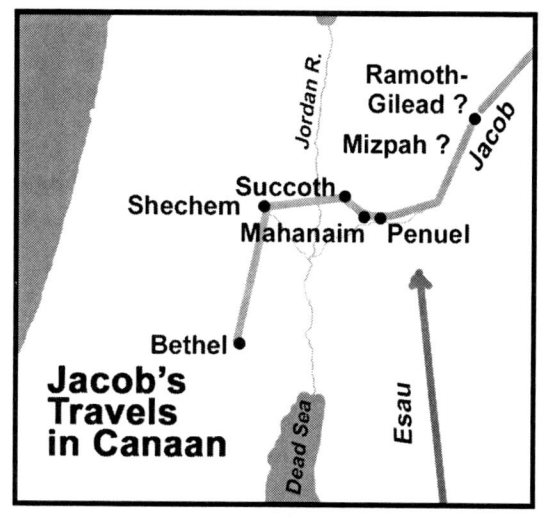

Q5. Why do we often fail to see God's blessings during the everyday conflicts of our lives? Why do blessings and conflicts so often come at the same time? What hope do we have in the midst of our struggles?

4. Jacob Wrestles with God and Man (Genesis 32-33)

Q1. (Genesis 32:1-2) Why does God reveal the angel army to Jacob? What is the significance of the presence of this army? Why do you think he calls the place Mahanaim ("two camps")?

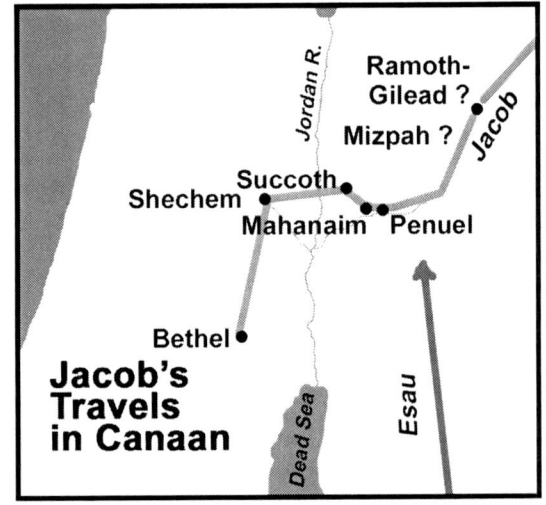

Q2. (Genesis 32.9-12) What does Jacob's prayer tell us about his fears? About his faith? About his pride? What are the signs of spiritual growth you see in Jacob since he left Canaan to go to Haran years before?

Q3. (Genesis 32:24-30) Who was the "man" Jacob wrestled with? What does the wrestling represent? Was it spiritual or physical? Why does the "man" wound Jacob permanently? What do you think the limp means to him?

Q4. (Genesis 33:1-16) How has Esau changed since Jacob had gone to Haran? How has Jacob changed? How does the encounter demonstrate Jacob's "craftiness"? How does it demonstrate his faith? Can Jacob be humble and "crafty" at the same time?

Copyright © 2010, Ralph F. Wilson <pastor@joyfulheart.com>. All rights reserved. Permission is granted to make one set of these participant handouts for each member of a local group or class at no charge.

5. Jacob Returns to Bethel (Genesis 33:17-35:29)

Q1. (Genesis 34) Why do you think Jacob is so silent after the rape of his daughter? What should he have done instead of being silent? What was right about the sons' reaction? What was wrong? What threat does the family now face if they stay in Shechem?

Q2. What happened when the Israelites disobeyed God and intermarried with the Canaanites? Why do you think God commanded them not to intermarry? Was this racial or spiritual or both? Why are Christians to marry "in the Lord"?

Q3. (Genesis 35:1-5) Why does Jacob's household need spiritual renewal? Why is it important to get rid of foreign gods? What do washing and putting on clean clothes represent? What "foreign gods" do you need to throw away? In what ways do you need to repent and lead a new, clean life?

Q4. (Genesis 35:9-15) Why do you think God appears to Jacob yet another time? What are the primary promises that God renews to Jacob?

Q5. (Genesis 35:22) What is the significance of Reuben's sin? In what way does it go beyond a sexual sin? We're not told, but how do you think this affected the family dynamics? Extra credit: Reuben has acted dishonorably here. In what ways does Reuben act honorably in the future? (37:21-29; 42:22, 37)?

6. Jacob's Depression, Fear, and Hope (Genesis 37-47)

Q1. (Genesis 37:31-35) What does bringing the blood-stained robe to Jacob say about these sons' attitude toward their father? How does this loss affect Jacob? How do you think it affects his future behavior?

Q2. (Genesis 42:35-43:14) What is Jacob's state of mind after the first trip to Egypt? If you were a psychologist, how would you diagnose him? What factors have paralyzed Jacob mentally and spiritually? Why do you think Jacob changed his mind about going again to secure grain?

Q3. (Genesis 45:4-8) Contrast Jacob and Joseph. Jacob has suffered great loss. Joseph has suffered great injustice. Why is Jacob's vision so bleak, but Joseph's so broad? What have been their differing responses to fear? What insight has kept Joseph from being bitter towards his brothers?

Q4. (Genesis 46:2-4) Faith is what quiets our fears. What in God's word to Jacob at Beersheba quiets his fears? God had brought the same assurance to Jacob before (28:15; 31:3). Why do you think he had stopped believing it? What is the relationship between faith and God's words?

Copyright © 2010, Ralph F. Wilson <pastor@joyfulheart.com>. All rights reserved. Permission is granted to make one set of these participant handouts for each member of a local group or class at no charge.

7. Jacob Offers Blessings (Genesis 46:28-49:33)

Q1. (Genesis 47:9) In what sense is life on earth like a "pilgrimage" or a journey with no permanent home? What happens to us when we settle down and get too comfortable with our lives? How do we retain a "journeying spirit" in our faith?

Ages in the Patriarchal Era

Nahor	119 years	(11:24)
Terah	205 years	(11:32)
Abraham	175 years	(25:7)
Isaac	180 years	(35:28)
Jacob	147 years	(47:28)
Joseph	110 years	(50:22)

Q2. (Genesis 48) Why does Jacob cross his hands when blessing Ephraim and Manasseh? Why does Joseph try to stop him? In what sense are Jacob's blessings an actual prophecy from God?

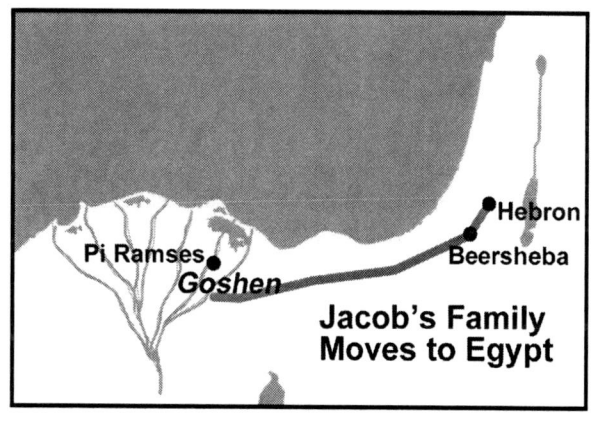

Q3. Why do we equate blessing with a lack of crisis in our lives? What are the effects of crises on our faith? How do they help us grow in our faith? Why do they sometimes destroy our faith?

Q4. (Genesis 48:15) How did God act as a Shepherd to Jacob? How does God act as a Shepherd to you? Do you trust him or rebel against his shepherding?

Copyright © 2010, Ralph F. Wilson <pastor@joyfulheart.com>. All rights reserved. Permission is granted to make one set of these participant handouts for each member of a local group or class at no charge.

CPSIA information can be obtained at www.ICGtesting.com
Printed in the USA
LVOW051424101111
254397LV00003B/34/P